My
Confirmation

My Confirmation

A Guide for Confirmation Instruction

Newly Revised and Updated

by
Thomas E. Dipko

United Church Press
Cleveland

Publisher's Note:

This book was first published in 1954 before the United Church of Christ was actually formed in 1957. It has well served our denomination's need for a confirmation resource and has been updated three times to better describe the church's current structures and actions in the world. This new edition has been revised by the Reverend Dr. Thomas E. Dipko. It includes revised and updated material since the 2000 Restructure.

United Church Press, 700 Prospect Avenue, Cleveland, Ohio 44115-1100
www.unitedchurchpress.com

Library of Congress Cataloging-in-Publication Data
My confirmation : a guide for confirmation instruction. – 4th ed.
        p.   cm.
        ISBN 0-8298-0991-0
        1. Confirmation-United Church of Christ-Study and teaching.
I. United Church of Christ
BX7475.5.C7M9   1994
264.05834082-dc20
                                                              94-8457
                                                              CIP
                                                              AC

Contents

Introduction: A New Venture   **1**

Part One— The Christian Guidebook   **5**

    1. What Is the Bible?   5

    2. How We Got Our Bible   9

    3. The Bible Story   19

    4. Using the Bible   24

Part Two—Christian Beliefs   **29**

    5. About God   29

    6. About Jesus   36

    7. About the Holy Spirit   50

    8. About Ourselves   53

    9. What We Believe   59

Part Three—The Christian Way of Life   **69**

    10. Christians Trust in God   69

    11. Christians Care for Others   77

    12. Christians Care for Themselves   85

    13. Christians Seek the Realm of God   92

Part Four—The Christian Church   97

    14. The Story of the Christian Church   97

    15. What Protestants Believe   111

    16. The Story of Our Denomination   114

    17. The Story of My Congregation   130

    18. The Church Service of Worship   134

    19. The Sacraments   141

Part Five—Christianity in Action   151

    20. The Work Our Denomination Is Doing   151

    21. The Church as Teacher   166

    22. The Church as Friend   172

    23. The Church as Missionary   179

Part Six—Some Questions to Face   189

    24. My Decision—What Will It Be?   189

    25. Why Do I Need the Church?   193

    26. Why Does the Church Need Me?   199

    27. What Does Confirmation Mean?   205

Resource Section   213

    The Contents of the Bible in Brief   213

    The Church Year   216

    The Span of Jesus' Life   218

    The Meaning of the Symbols on Page 220   219

    Bible Verses to Know   221

    Hymns Suitable for the Confirmation Service   222

    In a Church Member's Vocabulary   223

    Special Projects   232

    The Council for Health and Human Services Ministries   232

    Academies, Colleges, Universities, and Seminaries   232

Notes   234

Introduction:
A New Venture

You have joined this year's confirmation class. You are starting out on a new venture and you don't know just what to expect. What is confirmation anyway? Why does our church have it? Some churches don't.

What Is Confirmation?

Confirmation is the affirmation of baptism. Through baptism you entered (or will enter) the worldwide community of the Christian church. In confirmation you affirm this. You give yourself wholeheartedly to God and seek to know God's will for your life. You take Jesus as your Lord and Savior, whom you will follow all the days of your life. You let God's Holy Spirit guide you in all you do.

The word *confirm* means "to make firmer or stronger." When you are confirmed,

1. You will make firmer or stronger the baptismal vows taken for you (or that you took for yourself), and you will agree to live by them all your life.

2. God will make firmer and stronger claims on you.

3. Your membership in the church will be made firmer or stronger. For some of you, this will be the first time you will join in the Lord's Supper.

A good summary of confirmation is found in the answer to question 122 in the Evangelical Catechism: "Confirmation is the renewal of the baptismal covenant. The baptized children, having been instructed in the Christian faith, publicly confess their faith in their Savior Jesus Christ, promise obedience to [God] until death, and are received by the church into active membership."

Why Does Our Church Have It?

The act of confirmation is very old and very sacred. For many centuries boys and girls and men and women have become full members of the Christian church very much as you will when you are confirmed. Confirmation goes back to the time of the first-century church, when Christians were being persecuted in Jerusalem. Many left and went to other cities. Philip went to Samaria. There ... but you might as well read the story in your Bible. Turn to Acts 8:9–17. In Samaria, Peter and John "confirmed" the baptism given by Philip, and the people "confirmed" their faith in Jesus Christ.

In the early church confirmation came right after baptism, and there were two parts to the rite. In the first, the confirmand was anointed with oil; in the second, the minister prayed for the confirmand and laid hands on the confirmand's head. As the years went by, confirmation was usually separated from baptism, and the first part of the rite was used less and less. Our own church uses only the second part.

Most of you were baptized when you were babies. Your parents or guardians probably brought you to the church and there dedicated you to God. It was then that you "joined the church." But you were too young to make your own promises of loyalty, so your parents or guardians made them for you. Now you are old enough to make them for yourself.

Getting Ready for Confirmation

This book has been planned and written to help you get ready for confirmation. Look at the table of contents. As you read the chapter headings you will see that this book deals with some mighty important subjects. Take good care of this book and study it well. You will need to know its contents if you want to be a committed Christian and a good church member.

In addition to *My Confirmation* you will need the following to help you get ready for confirmation:

1. *A Bible.* The New Revised Standard Version is recommended.
2. *The hymnal* of your church.
3. *Other resources* such as a catechism, devotional books, and statements of faith, which your pastor will suggest.

Going to Church

Getting ready to be confirmed includes more than study, as you will discover as we go along. One matter needs to be mentioned now—going to church. You may or may not have been taking part in the church service of worship every Sunday. If you have not, now is the time to begin to form the habit of worshiping God in the company of other Christians. You should not miss a Sunday unless you are ill or have some equally good reason for being absent. But it is not enough just to be in attendance. You should go to church for the purposes of worshiping God and of getting from the service as much as you can for your daily living. The following suggestions may help you to achieve these purposes.

Enter the church reverently. This is not the time or place for talking to others. It is the time and place for worshiping God. When you have taken your place, bow your head and pray. Make up your own prayer, asking God to help you to be attentive so that the Holy Spirit may reach you as you worship, or use a prayer from the Bible, such as Psalm 19:14:

> *Let the words of my mouth and the meditation of my heart*
> *be acceptable to you,*
> *O Lord, my rock and my redeemer.*

Participate in every part of the service. To do this you will need to know the meaning of each part.

1.   If there is a *confession,* think over the words one by one. Think also of what you have done during the past week that is contrary to Christian teachings, and ask God to forgive you for your failings.

2.   During the *prayers,* turn your thoughts toward God and make the prayers your own. Use moments of silence, as well as the time during the prelude and the offertory, to think about God, to pray in your own words, and to open yourself to divine guidance.

3.   Sing the *hymns* thoughtfully. Think of the meaning of the words. When they are joyous, sing the hymns joyfully. If they form a prayer, sing the hymn quietly and prayerfully. If they are words of courage and faith, let them fill you with courage and faith as you sing.

4.   Try to get the main point of the *scripture* when it is read. Notice how often scripture is used throughout the service and how helpful it is as a call to worship, as a prayer, as a hymn, or as a blessing.

5. During the *offering*, think of the good the money will do, but as you give your money let it be a symbol of yourself. The giving of self to God is the heart of the offering service. Money is a real part of our life. As such, it is a suitable symbol for us to use in our offering to God. If you are not now giving regularly to the church out of your own money, this is the time to begin. Remember you are learning to stand on your own feet as a Christian, and that includes making your own offering.

6. Let the *special music* bring you its message. Anthems and other vocal numbers are prayers or hymns of praise to God, the words of which are often taken from the Bible. Sometimes they carry to the listener a special message that will help him or her to become a better Christian. Organ music or other instrumental music is chosen to arouse a certain mood: praise, adoration, prayer, or meditation. Look on those who sing or play as Christians who dedicate their talents to the service of God. Their singing or playing is another form of the offering of self to God.

Look for something in the sermon that will help you to be a better Christian. Not everything the minister says will apply to you. He or she must preach to all the people. He or she cannot talk to you alone. Nevertheless you can find, if you listen for it, something in the sermon that will help you to become more Christian.

Remain reverent throughout the service. There should be no letdown when the anthem is being sung or when the offering is being taken. When you truly and sincerely participate in the whole service you will find that the time is not too long to spend in worshiping God and in molding.

PART ONE
The Christian Guidebook

1

What Is The Bible?

All over the world at this moment people in many lands are reading the Bible in more than a thousand languages. In your own country each year it is listed as the best-seller among books. What is this book that commands the attention of so many people?

The Bible Is a Library

Most people think of the Bible as *a* book, even though they know that it has many parts written by many people.

In fact, the Bible is not one book, but sixty-six books bound together. The name *Bible* tells us, if we know what it means, that this book is really a library of smaller books. The word *bible* comes from a Greek word that is plural and that means "little books" or "booklets."

Turn to the page at the beginning of your Bible that lists the names of the books in the Old Testament (or Hebrew Scriptures). Hold your finger at this place and then find the list of names of the books in the New Testament. Now look at the two lists. You will notice that some of the books have strange names, such as Deuteronomy and Ecclesiastes. Others are named after the chief character in the book, such as Joshua or Ruth. Still others are named for the writer, such as Amos, Jeremiah, or Luke. Some are named for the people to whom they were written, such as Romans or Timothy.

Now look at the bookcase pictured on the next page. Notice that the books of the Bible group themselves into certain classifications. There are two main sections - the Old Testament and the New Testament. Each of these sections is divided into subdivisions. In the Old Testament there are four subdivisions: law, history, poetry, and prophecy. In the New Testament there are also four subdivisions: gospels (the word gospel means "good news"), history, epistles (which are letters), and revelation.

The Bible Is a Book

Despite these sections and subdivisions, the Bible is still thought of as a single book. Even though many people have had a hand in writing the sixty-six books that we call the Bible, there is a reason for putting them all between two covers and thinking of them as one.

There is a continuous story in the Bible, for all the books and all the writers show us how God from the very beginning has sought people to serve, and how they have tried to reach true communion with God—their Creator, Savior, and Guide. Furthermore, the story of the Old Testament leads into the New Testament as it tells of the birth of Jesus Christ into the world, of the good news of the coming of the realm of God among people, of Christ's sacrificial death on the cross, of his resurrection from the dead, and of the working of the Holy Spirit in the lives of people as they formed the church. You will read more of this story in chapter 3.

The Bible Contains the Word of God

When we say that the Bible contains the Word of God, we are saying that God speaks to us through the Bible. But how does God speak to us through this book?

1. *Through actions.* One of God's chief means of communicating with us is by the way God acts—the way the world is run, the way God treats people. The Bible tells us that the world was made by the Creator to be a good world. Read the first chapter of Genesis and underline lightly in your Bible the word *good* each time it is used. Write here the number of times you find the word. _____ The Bible tells us that God is good, just, forgiving, kind, loving, and self-giving in nature, and that God wants us to display these attributes.

2. *Through people who have lived close to the presence of God.* Because some people have come to know God in their experience, they can tell others about God's identity and will. Moses was such a person. The prophets were such people. But it is Jesus who has told us most about God's love and will. Jesus' whole life, as well as his death and resurrection, speak to us of God, for he was God's only child and so could be the perfect expression of God's

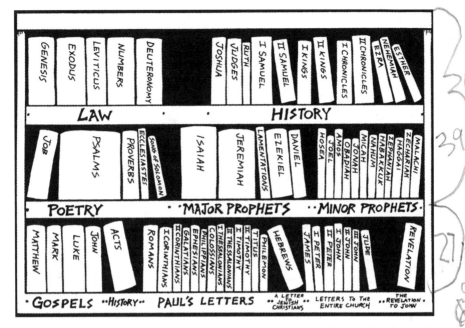

2014
39
27) New
5 16
66
39
27

nature. Jesus has given us a clear picture of what God is like, and he has told us how we must live if we want to be participants in the realm of God.

These people—those who wrote parts of the Bible, like Amos, or those about whom parts of the Bible were written, like Jesus—were inspired people. This means that God's Spirit was very close to them. (The words *inspired* and *spirit* look very much alike, do they not?) It also means that God could speak through them to other people. Through them God continues to speak to people; the Bible contains God's Word to us.

Facts You Should Know About the Bible

1. The word *bible* means ___little books___

2. The word *gospel* means ___the good news___

3. The word *epistle* means ___letters___

4. The Bible is divided into ___2___ parts; the ___Old testament___ and ___the new testanmen___ the _____

5. The Old Testament has ___39___ books; the New Testament, ___27___ books, which makes ___66___ books in the Bible.

6. The Old Testament contains all the biblical books written _before_ Jesus lived.

7. The New Testament contains all the biblical book written _after_ Jesus lived.

8. The story of the creation of the world is in _Genesis_

9. The story of Jesus is in _gospel_ .

10. The story of Paul is in _acts_ .

Match These

Place the letter of each name in the right-hand column before the correct statement in the left-hand column.

_m_ A great queen of the Hebrew people	**a.** Matthew
_d_ The last book in the Bible	**b.** Amos
_g_ A great missionary of the early church	**c.** Genesis
_a_ A book that tells of the life of Jesus	**d.** Revelation
_f_ The songbook of the Hebrews	**e.** David
_c_ The book that tells of the "beginnings"	**f.** Psalms
_b_ The prophet who said that God wants justice and righteousness above everything else	**g.** Paul
_i_ The first king of Israel	**h.** Sermon on the Mount
_j_ The book that tells the story of the early Christian church	**i.** Saul
_l_ Laws found in the book of Exodus	**j.** Acts of the Apostles
_h_ A sermon given by Jesus	**k.** The Good Samaritan
_k_ A parable of Jesus	**l.** The Ten Commandments
	m. Esther
	n. Ruth

2
How We Got Our Bible

There was a time when there was no Bible at all—no Ten Commandments, no Twenty-third Psalm, no Lord's Prayer. It was about three thousand years ago that the Bible began to be written. At that time there was no English language, no paper as we know it, no printing press. A thousand years or more passed by before the Bible was fully written, and even then much remained to be done before we could have an English Bible on our book-shelves. The story of how it got there is a wonderful one. Many people had a hand in it. God also had a hand in it.

Our Bible's Long Story

We can grasp the story best by breaking it up into periods of time. These periods are not all of the same length. Sometimes they overlap. The time line on the next page will help you to follow the story.

Period I
Songs and stories were repeated from parent to child

We must try to put ourselves now in the days from 1500 to 1000 years before Christ. When this period opened, the Israelites were not as yet settled in Palestine. They were nomads, wanderers. They lived in tents pitched near an oasis. Around them was the desert. They knew little or nothing about writing as yet. At nighttime they would gather around the campfire and sing songs they had heard from their parents before them. What would they sing? It may be that we still have some of their songs. Perhaps they sang the Song of

Our Bible's Long Story

Most dates are approximate

HISTORY		DATE	THE BIBLE	
The Hebrews wandering and settling down	Abraham, Isaac, Jacob	1500 B.C.	The Song of lamech The Song of the Well Stories of Abraham, Isaac, Joseph, Moses and his laws.	Songs and stories repeated from parent to child
	Moses	1300 B.C.		
The United Kingdom		1000 B.C.	Book of Jasher (lost) the First Histories	
		925 B.C.	Amos, Hosea, Micah,	The written Bible begun
	David	800 B.C,	Isaiah Jeramiah, other	
The Divided Kingdom			prophets	
		600 B.C.	Samuel, Kings	
Suffering in Exile	Jerusalem destroyed Return from exile	586 B.C. 536 B.C.	Ezekiel, Isaiah 40–55	Books of hope
In Palestine once more		150 B.C. 100 B.C.	Chronicles, Ezra, Nehemiah, Genesis to Joshua finished, Malachai, other prophets Job, Jonah, Ruth, Esther, Daniel; Proverbs and Psalms finished	The Old Testament finished
Beginnings of Christianity	Jesus, Paul	✚	Paul's letters, Gospels, etc.	The New Testament written
End of the persecutions	Constantine	100 300 400	Old Testament books selected New Testament books selected	The 66 Books of the Bible selected
The Dark Ages	The Crusades		Jerome translated Bible into Latin	The Bible greatly neglected
The Middle Ages		1,100		
Protestant Churches arise	Martin Luther	1382 1500 1611	Wycliff's translation Luther's translation King James Version	
Modern Era		1885 1901 1952 1961	English Revised Version American Standard Bible Revised Standard Version New English Bible New Testament	The Bible translated into modern languages (over 2,000)
		1970 1976 1989	New English Bible Today's English Version (The Good News Bible) New Revised Standard Version	

Lamech (Genesis 4:23–24) or the Song of the Well (Numbers 21:17–18). The children would listen and gradually learn these songs. Years later they would sing them to their children.

The early Israelites told stories also, stories they had heard from their parents. About whom did they tell? Why, Abraham and Sarah, of course, and Isaac, and Jacob, and Joseph. The children remembered the stories and told them later to their children. In Egypt some of these stories may have been written down on papyrus. (We get our word *paper* from this Egyptian word.)

As the Israelites made their way with much fighting into the Promised Land, they kept on singing old songs and telling old stories, and they added new ones. For example, they would surely tell again and again of Moses and his laws, or they would sing songs like the Song of Miriam (Exodus 15:21). In it all a careful listener would hear again and again the name of God, for they believed that God was with them in their going out and in their coming in.

What little writing was done in the days of desert wandering and while settling in Canaan was done on stone. (See Exodus 24:12; 31:18; and 34:1, 28; Deuteronomy 27:2–3; and Joshua 8:30–32.)

Period II
The written bible was begun.

This period covers almost another five hundred years — 1000–586 B.C. As it opens, we find the Hebrews fairly well settled in Palestine. David was their king, and he was uniting them into a strong nation. Not long afterward they began to make considerable use of writing. They wrote in Hebrew. They did not divide their writing into words as we do, nor did they write vowels. If we wrote as they did, the opening words of the Twenty-third Psalm would look like this:

THELRDSMSHPHRDSHLLNTWNT

Much of the Bible was written on skins, but some was written on papyrus.

A "book" in those days was not like those you know. It was a roll or scroll that was made by pasting sheets of skin or papyrus together. On this the scribes would write in narrow columns with a reed pen sharpened to a point and dipped in ink made from soot or charcoal. Turn to Jeremiah 36:18–23, 27–28, 32. These passages give a good picture of how that book of the Bible was written. (The penknife referred to in verse 23 was the knife used to keep the point of the reed pen sharp.)

The Bible does not contain all the books that were written in those days. Joshua 10:13 refers to another book, as does Numbers 21:14. Write the names of these other books here:

_____

_____

Around 800 B.C. two men, the one living in the south of Palestine and the other in the north, wrote two histories of Israel. These were later put together with some stories and law books to make the opening five or six books of our present Bible.

About 750 B.C. a prophet named Amos wrote down the message he believed God had given him for the people of Israel. This was the first book of our Bible to be written in its present form. A little later the prophet Isaiah spoke his messages and then wrote them down. At about the same time Hosea and Micah did the same.

A hundred years later, around 600 B.C., Jeremiah dictated his prophetic message (see Jeremiah 36). The books of Nahum, Habakkuk, and Zephaniah were written at about the same time. Around this time, too, some writers (or one writer) decided to teach the people a lesson through history. They used facts from existent history books (see 2 Kings 2:41; 14:19, 29) to write a history of their nation to show how God had had a hand in it. So 1 and 2 Samuel and 1 and 2 Kings were written. The Bible was growing.

Period III
Books of Hope Appeared

In 586 B.C. Jerusalem was destroyed by Nebuchadnezzar. Many Hebrews were exiled to Babylon. There they remained for about fifty years, and they were bitter years. It was hard for the exiles to keep up their hope and faith. It seemed that God had deserted them. Ezekiel and the writer of Isaiah 40–55 tried to encourage the people with preaching and writing. So the Bible continued to grow in these troubled times.

Period IV
The Old Testament was Finished

After the Jews returned to their war-scarred homes in Palestine, they had much to do to rebuild their nation, but the writing of the Bible went on. The last eleven chapters of Isaiah were written. The opening six or seven books of the Old Testament were finished—four hundred years after they were started. The last of the Hebrews' history—what is in 1 and 2 Chronicles, Ezra, and Nehemiah—was written.

The prophetic books—Malachi, Joel, Zechariah, Haggai — were added, as were the stories of Job, Jonah, and Ruth. Lamentations, the Song of Solomon, and Ecclesiastes took on their final form.

Two books made up of several collections of previous books—Proverbs and Psalms—were arranged as we know them today. Both of these had been taking shape for hundreds of years, from the times of David and Solomon.

Last of all, only about a hundred and fifty years before Jesus was born, Esther and Daniel were added. Now the Old Testament was finished.

Period V
The New Testament was Written

The only Bible Jesus had was the Old Testament—the Hebrew Scriptures— but his life inspired a new group of people, called Christians, who added a whole new part to the Bible. The books poured forth so fast that the New Testament was written in only about one-fifteenth of the time it took to write the Old Testament.

The New Testament was begun when Paul sat down in Corinth one day around A.D. 50 (only twenty or so years after the close of Jesus' early life) to write a letter to the Christians of Thessalonica. We know this letter as 1 Thessalonians. From then until his death (probably in A.D. 64) Paul wrote many other letters to the churches that he established and to his friends and coworkers.

In the meantime, people who had known Jesus personally had been writing down for those who had not been with Christ some of the things that Jesus had said and done (see Luke 1:1-2). But it was not until somewhere around the year A.D. 70 that the first of our Gospels was written to give a complete story of the life of Jesus. This was the Gospel of Mark. Matthew, Luke, and John followed within the next thirty years.

Luke decided to add a history of the early church and the story of Paul to his life of Christ. We know it as the Acts of the Apostles.

The books we have mentioned thus far make up a large part of the New Testament. About one hundred years after Jesus' crucifixion and resurrection, everything we now have in our New Testament was written. So far as actual writing was concerned, the Bible was now finished.

Period VI
The Bible was Completed

From a large number of religious books written by the Hebrews and the early Christians sixty-six books were selected for our Bible. These books had stood the test of time and use. Through them, people of all ages had come to know God and God's will. Through these books God had spoken to them.

So far as the Old Testament was concerned, the business of selecting began long before Jesus. About 400 B.C. the five opening books had been agreed upon. But it was not until A.D. 100 that the thirty-nine books of the Old Testament were finally chosen.

As the early Christians met in little groups for worship, they read from the Hebrew Scriptures, but in time they also began to read from the new Christian writings. As more and more was written, it was clear that some selection would have to be made to be sure that the churches had writings that were truly inspired by God and worthy to become part of the sacred scriptures. The four Gospels were probably selected first. There was considerable debate about including 2 Peter and 2 and 3 John. But by A.D. 400 the church was fairly certain that our present twenty-seven books—no more and no less—were worthy of being in the New Testament.

Some of the books that were rejected contained such useful and good information that many editions of the Bible have carried them in a separate section called the Apocrypha. You may have heard of 1 and 2 Esdras, Judith, Baruch, Susanna, 1 and 2 Maccabees, or some of the others. Some Bibles may have these books. They have also been printed in a separate book called The *Apocrypha.*

Period VII
The Bible was Greatly Neglected

During a period called the Middle Ages, the Bible was not widely used, although scribes continued to copy it by hand. A man named Jerome, living at the beginning of this period, translated the Bible into Latin. (The Old Testament had been written in Hebrew and translated into Greek. The New Testament had been written in Greek.) This translation was called the Vulgate (meaning "common") because it was in the language that was common at that time.

Period VIII
Modern-language Bibles Appeared

In time, Latin was no longer the language used by the common people, and they could not understand what was being said in the church services. So people began to translate parts or all of the Bible into the language that they could understand. Martin Luther translated it into German. Others translated it into other languages. Now parts of the Bible can be read in over a thousand tongues.

The man who first put the whole Bible into our own language was John Wyclif. This he did over a hundred years before Columbus sailed to America.

Another great English translator was William Tyndale. In 1525 he gave us the first *printed* English New Testament—but what a price he paid! He was driven from England to the continent of Europe, hunted from place to place, and finally both strangled and burned in Belgium. You might be interested to see how he translated Hebrews 1:1–2:

> God in tyme past diversely and many wayes, spake vnto the fathers by prophets: but in these last dayes he hath spoken vnto vs by hys sonne, whom he hath made heyre of all things: by whom also he made the worlde.

Note that this passage is not divided into verses. The division of the Bible into verses came soon after Tyndale's day.

The English translation that has been used by the largest number of people is the King James Version, so called because King James I of England appointed fifty scholars to prepare a Bible that would suit the different churches in England at that time and correct inaccuracies in the current versions. These people worked three and a half years and brought out their version in 1611.

By the middle of the nineteenth century, it became apparent that changes were needed in this version. It had to be brought up to date in language. Archaeology had revealed new facts about the times in which the Bible was written. Ancient Hebrew and Greek had come to be understood better. So in 1885 the Revised Version was published. In the United States, scholars made further changes and published the American Standard Version in 1901.

Since then a number of scholars have brought out their own translations. Among the better known are *The Bible: A New Translation* by James Moffatt, 1926 and *The Complete Bible—An American Translation,* New Testament by Edgar J. Goodspeed, *Old Testament* by J. M. Prowis Smith, 1927.

Because of the many discoveries of ancient biblical manuscripts and other archaeological findings, and because modern Americans cannot always understand the real meaning of the Bible when old English is used, churches in the United States authorized the preparation of a new translation for our times. Thirty-two scholars with an advisory board of fifty denominational representatives (including our own) were set to work on the colossal task. For years this committee worked, bringing out the New Testament in 1946; in 1952, they completed the Revised Standard Version of the Bible.

Within the first eight weeks after publications, 1.6 million copies of the Revised Standard Version were sold. Many people began to read the Bible with new understanding and appreciation. Because of its faithfulness to the original languages and its careful scholarship, the Revised Standard Version gained acceptance among fundamentalists and, with some changes and additions, was approved for use by Roman Catholics and Eastern Orthodox Christians.

The New English Bible (New Testament only) came out in 1961 (the complete Bible was published in 1970). It was prepared by a group of British scholars. Like the Revised Standard Version, this new translation was widely welcomed. Today's English Version (the Good News Bible) was completed in 1976 as a modern translation in "today's English." It has gained wide acceptance, especially among young people (and is preferable to the Living Bible, which is a paraphrase, not a translation).

Does this close the long story of our Bible? Not by any means. In a sense the Bible is still growing, not in size, but in our understanding of it. Just before the Old Testament in the complete Revised Standard Version was published, some very ancient scrolls, including some of the Old Testament books, were discovered in a cave near the Dead Sea. These scrolls were older than any other manuscripts that we have of the Bible. They had been placed in this cave one hundred years before Jesus was born. The Isaiah scroll was especially helpful to the members of the Old Testament committee as they tried to make their translation as accurate as possible. But since the publication of the Revised Standard Version even more valuable findings have been made.

In 1989, the New Revised Standard Version of the Bible appeared. Once again, drawing from an ecumenical committee and incorporating the latest in Biblical scholarship and a sensitivity to inclusive language, this translation continues the extraordinary tradition of rendering God's word accessible to people everywhere.

The Hand of God Is Still Writing

Someone remarked how strange it was that so many archaeological discoveries should be made of ancient Bible manuscripts and other items throwing light on the Bible just when a new version of the Bible was being prepared. "Not at all strange," was the reply of one of the scholars who had a hand in deciphering the Dead Sea Scrolls, "the hand of God is still writing the Bible."

What has been said in the last few pages about the part that people have played in writing, selecting, copying, translating, and studying the Bible does not mean that God did not have a hand in it. God was guiding and directing these people through the Holy Spirit as they worked to interpret to each generation the will of God.

God seeks to communicate with us, and in the Bible we can learn of God and God's work in the world. To emphasize this point, reread "The Bible Contains the Word of God" on page 6.

The Story of the Bible

1. There was no Bible _____ years ago.

2. The Bible was first spoken by people in the form of _____ and _____.

3. The books of the Bible were written on _____ of animals and on _____.

4. The first book in the Bible to be written was _____.

5. The book of _____ is known as the hymnbook of the Hebrews.

6. Wise sayings of people like Solomon are in the book of _____.

7. The Old Testament was written in the _____ language.

8. The first book of the New Testament to be written was a _____.

9. The New Testament was written in the _____ language.

10. The first of our four Gospels to be written was by _____.

_____

11. The Bible was written by people who were _____by God.

12. The person who translated the Bible into Latin was _____

13. _____copied Bibles by hand in monasteries during the Middle Ages.

14. The one who first translated the whole Bible into English was _____.

15. The one who printed the first Bible in English was _____.

16. The Bible translation that was made by fifty scholars in 1611 is called the _____.

17. The version of the Bible that was published in full text in 1952 is the

_____.

18. Other versions and translations of the Bible into modern English are

_____

_____

_____.

3

The Bible Story

If someone were to ask you to give a brief summary of the Bible, how would you do it? Perhaps you would simply say that it cannot be done. After all, in our English versions the Bible comes to well over a thousand pages, and there are sixty-six different books bound within its covers. These were written in various languages, in various places, and over a period of at least a thousand years. It would be easier perhaps to give a summary of each of the books than to try to summarize them all together.

But there is a continuous story that runs through the Bible, a very dramatic story. Although the plot may not be too clear in some of the books, most of the biblical writers seem to be aware of the great drama of which they are writing. When an ancient Israelite wanted to state his or her creed, he or she told a story of how God had brought Abraham and Sarah out of Mesopotamia and had led their descendants down into Egypt; when harsh treatment came, God delivered them from Egypt and brought them into a land flowing with milk and honey. This was the God in whom they believed. If you want to read this very early confession of faith, you will find it in Deuteronomy 26:5–9 and in Joshua 24:2–13.

When the first Christians wanted to confess their faith, they also told a story. It was the story of how God had come to them in Jesus. You will find it in Acts 10:36–41. As you read it you will discover that when we join in the Apostles' Creed today, we tell about the same story.

The Story of Salvation

We see, then, that the authors in both the Old Testament and the New Testament told a story, and that the leading character in each story was none other than God. But it was not a story about God alone. It was the story of the way God had acted to save people. In the Old Testament they were saved from oppression and slavery in Egypt. In the New Testament they were saved from bondage to sin and from fear of death. For this reason, we can say that the story that the whole Bible tells is the story of salvation. As a matter of fact, we can divide it into a two-act drama with a prologue and an epilogue. The prologue is in the first three chapters of Genesis. We find Act I in the Old Testament; Act II covers the New Testament. The epilogue, or conclusion, is in the last book of the New Testament, Revelation.

In this chapter we can suggest only the major scenes in the Bible story. Once we have clear in our minds the whole sweep of the biblical drama, we can begin to see how each part fits into the whole story. This in turn may help us to fix in our minds the part of the story contained in the major books of the Bible.

Prologue

In the opening chapters of Genesis (Genesis 1–3) we have two accounts of creation, one written about 900 B.C. and the other about 500 B.C. Both tell us that "in the beginning" God created the world of nature and made humanity in the divine image. We see here that the scene of the biblical story is the world. More than that, the chief characters are also introduced, namely, God and people. The story of the garden in chapters 2 and 3 suggests that people were created to be in close fellowship and personal relationship with God. But humanity rebelled against God by disobeying. The rest of the Bible reveals how great our separation is from God and how God acts to restore us to fellowship.

Act I

The Old Testament tells the story of how God called a people to a special relationship. This people, the Israelites, were to express this relationship through the following actions:

1. Obeying God's commandments
2. Receiving and cherishing the revelation of God through the prophets and in the people of Israel
3. Being "a light to the nations" (Isaiah 49:6)

But Israel disobeyed God's commandments; it persecuted the prophets and it despised the Gentiles. Because of this, both the northern and southern territories were destroyed and the people were taken to Babylon in exile. After nearly fifty years of captivity, a remnant of the people returned and attempted a new beginning. As Act I comes to a close, even the remnant had failed to grasp God's purpose for Israel. It had become a nation in search of a soul.

Scene 1. ***God and the Early Beginnings of Humankind.*** In the story of Cain and Abel and in the account of the flood we see that from the very outset of human history, it was sin that separated people from God. The story of Noah reveals that God desires to enter into a covenant relationship (Genesis 4-11).

Scene 2. ***The Foreparents of Israel.*** This part of the story tells of Abraham and Sarah, Isaac, and Jacob. It ends with the settling of the house of Jacob in Egypt after Joseph had risen to a high position under the reigning Pharaoh (Genesis 12-50).

Scene 3. ***Oppression and the Deliverance from Egypt.*** After years of oppression and slavery God sent a deliverer whose name was Moses. Under his leadership the people escaped (Exodus 1-15). At Mount Sinai the people entered into a covenant with God. The terms of the covenant are the Ten Commandments (Exodus 20:1-17). As the people wandered in the wilderness and prepared to enter the Promised Land, Moses gave them more laws (Exodus, Leviticus, Numbers, Deuteronomy).

Scene 4. ***Entering and Settling the Land of Canaan.*** Joshua led the Israelites to victory over the Canaanites, and the people settled down. For a while there were voluntary leaders like Deborah, Gideon, and Samson, who were called judges (Joshua, Judges).

Scene 5. ***The Rise of the Monarchy: Samuel, Saul, and David.*** In this period there was an attempt to unify the people of Israel, not only politically, but also religiously. Both Saul and David tried to rally the people around God (1 and 2 Samuel, 1 Chronicles).

Scene 6. ***The Division into Two Territories.*** Although Solomon built a beautiful temple to the one God, he oppressed the people and tolerated the worship of foreign gods. The northern tribes revolted and the people were divided into two nations: Israel in the north, and Judah in the south. Despite the warnings of prophets like Isaiah, Amos, Hosea, and Micah, the rulers and people of the northern territory deserted God and worshiped Canaanite deities. The prophets saw that God had no alternative but to destroy Israel. Judah alone remained of this once great people. Jeremiah and Ezekiel attempted to lead Judah back to trust in God. But Judah put its trust in chariots of war and was also destroyed (1 and 2 Kings, 2 Chronicles).

Scene 7. *God's People in a Strange Land.* Taken into exile in Babylon, many of the people gave up hope of ever returning. Some even gave up their faith. But others like Ezekiel and the unknown prophet who wrote chapters 40–66 of the book of Isaiah spoke words of promise and encouraged the people to return and build a new Israel.

Scene 8. *The Return from Exile and the Rebuilding of Jerusalem and the Temple.* When the opportunity presented itself; the Hebrews returned from exile and began the arduous task of rebuilding. The prophets Haggai and Zechariah encouraged them. The psalms were collected for use in the worship of the temple. Later on, Ezra and Nehemiah led the people in rebuilding the city wall and in adopting the Law.

Scene 9. *A Nation in Search of Its Calling.* The nation was reestablished under Persian domination. The temple became the center of Jewish life and the Law its guide. Nevertheless, the people still failed to see why God had called them. There was a great debate over the Gentiles. A few people, like the writers of Ruth and Jonah, believed that God cared even for Israel's enemies and that some good could come from Gentiles. But Ezra, Obadiah, and the author of Esther looked down on non Jews and urged the nation to separate itself from foreigners.

Some thinkers in Judah had begun to wonder whether God had really chosen Israel after all.

Act II

The second act in the story of salvation (the New Testament) tells how God fulfilled the continuing purpose and the hope of ancient Israel in Jesus and the church. The long debate about the relationship between Israel and other peoples came to an end. By sending Jesus, God made clear how God's children are not to come from any particular nation, but from all nations and races. They are to come together into the church and by their love and worship show all humankind the way to God. Thus we find ourselves taking part in the drama of salvation. Just as those who first heard the preaching of the apostles responded in faith and entered the new relationship with God (the new covenant), so we hear them speaking to us today, reminding us of our responsibilities as members of the church of Jesus Christ.

Scene 1. ***Jesus with the People.*** This is the climax of the Bible story, for it tells of the coming of the long-awaited Redeemer. The prophets had dreamed of the Messiah, and the people had longed for deliverance. But those who lived during the reign of Caesar Augustus did not recognize Jesus. He was born in an obscure village of Palestine. He grew up as any village boy might. For just the final two years of his life he went about preaching, teaching, healing, and seeking followers. He got into trouble with the religious authorities and was crucified. But then something happened that electrified his followers. They discovered that the Jesus who they thought was dead was risen and was present with them. They recognized him as God's Son, sent by God to establish the realm of love among people (Matthew, Mark, Luke, John).

Scene 2. ***The Church of Jesus Christ.*** The early Christians firmly believed that in Jesus' life and teachings and in his death and resurrection God had shown love for humanity and had called a new people to service. Therefore it was important to tell the story of Jesus' life to those who were not members of the Christian community and to challenge them to follow Jesus as their Savior. The book in the Bible entitled Acts of the Apostles tells how apostles and missionaries like Peter, Stephen, Philip, and Paul laid the foundations of the church and helped to spread Christianity from Jerusalem to Rome and beyond. The story of salvation was told through missionaries; through letters by such men as Paul, James, Peter, and John; and through the lives of courageous Christians as they lived and died in the sure knowledge that their sins would be forgiven and they would live forever if they put their trust in God and in Jesus Christ.

Epilogue

The conclusion of the drama is found in the book of Revelation. This is not an easy book to understand, but it is clear that the writer was saying that just as history began with God (Genesis 1-3), so God will be at the end of history. No one knows exactly when it will end or how it will end, but all Christians agree that history will not just run down as a clock runs down, but that God's realm will come in all its fullness. John's vision of this rule is in Revelation 21.

4

Using the Bible

Benjamin Franklin once said to a young man, "My advice to you is that you cultivate an acquaintance with and a firm belief in the Holy Scriptures."

Oliver Cromwell, the great English Puritan, when quite ill, read Philippians 4:11–13, after which he remarked, "That scripture did once save my life, when my eldest son Robert died."

These two men had evidently learned how to use the Bible in everyday life. Through it God could speak to them and guide them. People who have learned to use the Bible correctly are usually strong people, strong in the knowledge that they are doing God's will and that God's Spirit is working in them.

How Much Do You Use the Bible?

If all the Bibles were to be taken out of your home, your neighbor's home, your pastor's home, your church, your community, the nation—would it make any difference? Could you get along just as well without the Bible as with it? Many people think they could.

If you don't read the Bible regularly, or if you don't get much help from your reading, why don't you?

Is it because the language seems old to you and you can't understand what it says? Maybe you need a copy of the New Revised Standard Version or Today's English Version, which are in modern American English.

Is it because it talks about people who lived two or three thousand years ago in lands on the other side of the earth and you can't see any sense in studying about them? You ask, How can what they did then help me now? Keep in mind that these people learned many lessons about life and about God that we need to know if we are to live abundant lives.

Is it because the Bible was written by adults, to adults, and for the most part about grown men and women? How can such a book help you, a teenager, to get along with your peers? Remember that the principles for good living are the same for all ages.

Is it because you don't know how to find your way around the Bible to get to the parts you need at a particular time? A first step toward being able to use the Bible intelligently is to learn the names of the sixty-six books in their proper order and to know in general what they contain. You will find a brief statement of the contents of each book on pages 213–216. Underlining passages that have special meaning for you is helpful too. Making a list of passages for use when you feel blue or discouraged, when you are afraid, when you are extremely happy, when you are sad, and when you feel almost any emotion may aid you in your devotions.

Is it because the Bible looks so big, and the usual way to read a book is to begin at the beginning and continue to the end? Remember that the Bible is made up of sixty-six books, and, while it is good occasionally to read a whole book through in one sitting, smaller parts of the Bible may be read to great advantage.

How to Read the Bible

There are many ways of reading the Bible. Seven are mentioned here. Which of these ways are best for you?

1. *Read the Bible through from start to finish.* There are 1189 chapters in the Bible. If you read three chapters a day and five each Sunday, you will finish the Bible in a year with a few days to spare. Most people think that this is not the best way to get help from the Bible. It is too mechanical.

2. *Read it a book at a time.* The Gospel of Mark can be read through in one afternoon. Amos, Philippians, and other books are much shorter. To get the most out of such reading, one really ought to know when the book was written, where, by whom, to whom, and the like.

3. *Read its beautiful and helpful passages.* This is probably the way most people read the Bible. They have favorite passages to which they turn again and again. Some of the finest are the following:

Exodus 20:1-17	The Ten Commandments
Psalm 23	"The Lord is my shepherd"
Psalm 46	"God is our refuge and strength"
Psalm 121	"I lift up my eyes to the hills"
Isaiah 53	"Surely he has borne our infirmities"
Matthew 5-7	The Sermon on the Mount
John 14	"Do not let your hearts be troubled"
1 Corinthians 13	The chapter on love
Romans 12	"I appeal to you therefore, brothers and sisters, by the mercies of God"

Many Christians know large parts of these passages by heart and so have them ready to use when they want or need them.

4. *Read it along with those who use the Revised Common Lectionary.* A lec-*tionary* is a list of three readings and a Psalm for each Sunday of the year and for special days in the church calendar, like Epiphany or Ash Wednesday. In addition, for daily readings that relate to this lectionary, you may use *Around the Sundays.* Reading in this manner will unite you with millions of Christians who are reading parts of the Bible on the same day.

5. *Read it along with your church school courses.* If done during the week, each class session will mean a great deal more. Studying according to a plan with the help of your teacher will give you a knowledge and an understanding of great portions of the Bible that will stand you in good stead during our life.

6. *Read it along with other books, such as* How the Bible Came to Us *by Meryl Doney.* Books like this one help to open up the Bible for us and make it far more interesting.

7. *Read it along with a plan of daily prayer.*

8. *Read it for the help you need at the moment.* This is probably the best way of all, for you will get from its pages what so many Christians before you have gotten—help, strength, guidance, comfort, faith, hope, and love. Jesus himself used his Bible for this purpose. Read Matthew 4:1—11 to see how he uses scripture to help him in the time of temptation. Read also Matthew 27:46. Here Jesus is quoting the first verse of Psalm 22 in his agony on the cross. Read this psalm and see why he would use this psalm at such a time.

Bible Passages that Help

The following passages may help you—

In time of trouble

Psalm 42:5 _____

_____

Romans 8:28 _____

_____

When you have done something wrong

Isaiah 55:7 _____

_____

1 John 1:8–9 _____

_____

When someone you love has died

John 11:25–26 _____

_____

John 14:1–2 _____

_____

When you are tempted to do something wrong

Hebrews 4:15–16 _____

_____

James 1:12–15 _____

_____

When you have an "enemy"

Matthew 5:43–46 _____

_____

Matthew 18:21–22 _____

_____

When you are very thankful and happy

Psalm 103:1–2_____

_____

Psalm 150 _____

_____

When you are not sure what the right way of life is

Micah 6:8 _____

_____

Matthew 25:31–46 _____

_____

PART TWO
Christian Beliefs

5
About God

The next several chapters have to do with what we as Christians believe. Some people say that it doesn't matter what we believe; we need only to live good, true, and useful lives. It is what a person does, not what she or he believes, that counts. But this is hardly true, for what a person truly believes has much to do with how she or he lives. Suppose that of two persons living side by side, the one believed in a god who loved and cared for all people and the other believed in no god at all. Do you think you could tell which was which? By what signs might you be able to identify a person who believes in a god and one who does not?

God

God is a very simple word of three letters, which we say quite easily. Do we know what it means? Who is God? What does God look like? Can God be seen at all? Where? In outer space somewhere? Inside us speaking to us in our consciences? In the trees making them put forth leaves in springtime? What does God do? Does God care about us at all? Does God hear us when we pray? Does God know what we are thinking about in this time and place?

What the Bible Says About God

God has been trying to reveal the fullness of life and love to all people for a long, long time, and they in turn have been thinking about God. We may well begin by trying to find out what they have said. Write in your own words the ideas about God in the following passages from the Bible:

Deuteronomy 6:4 _____

Psalm 25:8 _____

Psalm 90:4 _____

Psalm 139:1–4 _____

Psalm 139:7–12 _____

Isaiah 42:5 _____

Matthew 6:8–9 _____

Luke 12:6 _____

John 4:24 _____

John 14:9 _____

Ephesians 4:6 _____

James 1:17 _____

1 John 1:5 _____

1 John 3:1 _____

1 John 4:8 _____

1 John 4:12 _____

1 John 5:20 _____

What, Then, Do We Believe About God?

There are many, many true ideas about God. Perhaps we can gather up the most important ones in six statements.

1. *God is spirit.* We cannot see God. However, we can see God at work in the world in the beauties and marvels of nature and in the lives of loving persons. These we can see, but no one has seen God in all the fullness of personhood. Being spirit, God is everywhere.

2. *God is the Creator of all things.* Everything was made by God. It did not just happen. God made it and, we believe, made it for our happiness and well-being. Everything we have comes from God. There is nothing of which we can possibly think that did not come from God.

Sometimes we think that we create things, but we merely use things that God has created. For instance, we have learned how to split the atom and to use this knowledge in many ways, but it is God who created the atom with all its possibilities.

God is a great God, and all powerful. Only such a power could have made this universe and could govern it day by day. God's knowledge is as great as God's power.

3. *God is good.* Because God is good, God wants us to be good. When we are bad, sooner or later this badness does not work. This is because a good God has made our world, and goodness will work in it but badness will not. It takes a long time for this to prove itself in some cases, but it always does.

4. *God is a loving parent.* Jesus used the word Father time and time again. We can go to God as children go to their parents. We can talk to God and be listened to. God loves us and cares for each one of us—more than the best parent who ever lived. God has the same kind of plans and hopes for our world that a good parent has for his or her family. God wants us all to be happy and good and to live together as brothers and sisters.

5. *God is like Jesus.* This is our finest Christian belief about God. When we want to know what God is like, we stop first to recall what Jesus was like—brave, kind, caring for all, sorry when others went wrong. We then say that God is like that.

6. *God is more than we can know or think.* God is very great, and we are small. When we have done our best to imagine God's greatness, it is beyond that. When we have done our best to imagine how good God is, God is beyond that. There is only one fitting way to speak to or about God—and that is with deep reverence.

Read the Statement of Faith on pages 60–61 and think about what it affirms concerning God's activity.

Some Questions About God

Where is God? A little boy once said to his mother that God came down a ladder into their backyard to make the roses grow. Was this right? Can God come "down"? Is God "up"? One of the Russian cosmonauts said that he did not see God in outer space when he was circling the earth. Should he have expected to "see" God? Or is God everywhere all the time, just as you are all through your body all the time? What do you think?

Why does God allow people to suffer? This is a question that has been troubling humankind for many centuries, and it is hard to answer. The book of Job in our Bible is about this question. If God is really good, why does God let people, especially good people, suffer?

In a junior high church school class some boys and girls were wondering about this question. John said that a lot of suffering is caused by people themselves. A man becomes drunk, drives his car into a tree alongside the road, and spends painful months in a hospital. God did not do that. The man brought it on himself. Michael wasn't satisfied with this. He said he believed God deliberately sent suffering at times to punish people for their sins. He had heard of a woman who was as dishonest as anyone could imagine, and—sure enough!—her house burned down one night. Wasn't that God's doing?

But this didn't satisfy Angela at all. She said, "What about the thousands of abused children who suffer? The countless people whose property is destroyed by war? They suffer terribly. They did nothing to bring on this suffering. They did not deserve such a punishment from God. Why should they have to suffer? If God is a loving parent, why is this allowed to happen?"

"Well," said Jasmine, "their suffering is caused in the long run by the hatred and selfishness in people's hearts. And God can't stop that right off, so long as we're allowed to choose between right and wrong. I can more or less understand that. But what gets me is the suffering caused by an earthquake, by cancer, or by AIDS. Why does God allow that? Is it because we need some hardships for our own good?"

What Do You Think?

What is meant by "God in three Persons, blessed Trinity?" We sing these words every time we sing the hymn "Holy, Holy, Holy." What do they mean? How can there be three Persons in one God? Many pastors open the Sunday morning service by saying, "In the name of the Father, and of the Son, and of the Holy Spirit" (or "In the name of the Creator, the Redeemer, and the Sustainer"). What does this mean? Is the Holy Spirit different from God?

To answer these questions is not easy. Perhaps the best answer is this: God meant so much to the early Christians that they could not put all that God meant to them into one word or statement. They knew God as the Creator of all the earth and the Parent of all humankind. That was God the Parent. But then this same God who had made all things was embodied most clearly in Jesus Christ. That was God the Child. But after Jesus' earthly life was over, the Spirit of God who had made everything and whom they had seen in Jesus was still with them—they were sure of it! That was God the Spirit.

When the early Christians used the word *trinity* they did not mean three gods at all. The Latin *trinitas* means "three in one." When they spoke of three Persons they did not mean three separate individuals. The word person comes from the Latin word *persona*—which first meant the mask an actor wore on the stage in those times, then the actor himself, and finally a separate individual. So when Christians first used the word person, a part at least of their meaning was that the one God had come to them in three different roles, just as one actor can play three different parts, or as one woman can be a daughter, wife, and a mother at the same time. They meant more than this, but they did not mean three separate gods. All of this is clearly stated in the Athanasian Creed, which was drawn up about six hundred years after Christ and reads in part as follows:

> So the Father is God, the Son is God, and the Holy Ghost
>   is God.
> And yet they are not three Gods, but one God.
> So likewise the Father is Lord, the Son Lord, and the
>   Holy Ghost Lord.
> And yet not three Lords, but one Lord.
> And in this Trinity none is before, or after another; none
>   is greater, or less than another.
> But the whole three Persons are coeternal together,
>   and coequal.

So when you come across some mention of the Trinity— Father, Son, and Holy Spirit or Creator, Redeemer, and Sustainer—it can mean to you that Christians believe in one God who as Parent made all things, as Child showed personhood to lead people away from their sins into a full life, and as Spirit is even now at work in the world and in our own hearts.

How the Bible Describes God

Fill in the following blanks with one or more words from the scripture passages listed.

_____ Genesis 17:1

_____ Deuteronomy 33:27

_____ Psalm 99:9

_____ Psalm 119:137

_____ Ecclesiastes 12:1

_____ Isaiah 63:16a

_____ Nahum 1:7

_____ John 4:24

_____ 1 John 1:9

_____ 1 John 4:8

True or False?

Indicate with a T if the statement is true, with an F if false.

_____ 1.   One cannot see God because God is spirit.

_____ 2.   God created everything in the world except people.

_____ 3.   God is all-powerful and knows all things.

_____ 4.   God can do no wrong.

_____ 5.   God loves only those who do the divine will.

_____ 6.   Whatever Jesus is like, God is like also.

_____ 7.   God loves and cares for us all the time.

_____ 8.   God gives us everything that we pray for.

_____ 9.   God always sends suffering to punish people for their sins.

_____ 10.   God allows us to choose between right and wrong.

The Trinity

You will find in each pair of scripture passages one or more words that are the same. Write these in the blanks.

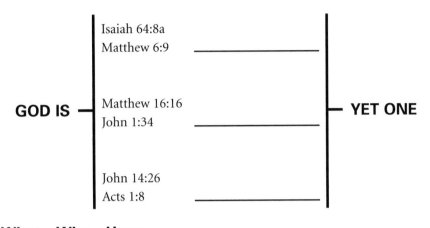

GOD IS

Isaiah 64:8a
Matthew 6:9 _____

Matthew 16:16
John 1:34 _____

John 14:26
Acts 1:8 _____

YET ONE

What—Why—How

Answer the following questions in your own words.

What about God is like Jesus?

Why does God allow people to suffer?

How can we live the kind of life that God wants us to live?

6

About Jesus

Unfortunately, we have no photographs of Jesus. There were no cameras in those days. None of the artists who have painted him ever saw him or even had a photograph of him. Some of them have probably given us the wrong idea of him, without meaning to do so. They have been so anxious to show him as being kind and gentle (which of course he was) that they left out other characteristics. But many artists today are not concerned about what Jesus looked like. They are trying to help people know what Jesus means to us.

Knowing About Jesus

The first step in coming to love and follow Jesus is to learn to know him as a person. We can't love someone unless we know him or her. One way in which we learn to know Jesus is to read about him in the Bible. Sometime before you are confirmed you should read each one of the Gospels. These contain his life story. Then test yourself on the facts of his life. Turn to page 41 and fill in the blanks in the story. Check your answers with the Bible references given. Make sure you know the story of Jesus well.

Then imagine what he would be like if he were walking the earth today. Let's ask some questions with all reverence:

Would he be strong, or weak?

Would you be afraid to go near him?

With what kind of people would he spend his time—good people? bad people? people of your own race? people of other races? rich people? poor people? Americans? Russians? Christians? Jews?

How might he earn his living?

What would he make you think about: God? Church? Money? Success? Being kind and thoughtful?

What would he like most about your community? your church? your nation? yourself? What would he dislike about any of these?

What are some of the things he would spend his time on? Are there any things you can't picture him as doing?

Names by Which Jesus Is Known

Two verses in the New Testament contain five important names for Jesus. Mark 1:1 says, "The beginning of the gospel of *Jesus Christ, the Son of God*;" John 13:13 says, "You call me *Teacher* and *Lord*; and you are right, for so I am" (italics added).

Jesus. This was the name given him as a baby. It was given to other babies also. It is the Greek way of writing *Joshua* which means "Jehovah is salvation," or more simply, "God saves us." So when we call Jesus *Savior*, we are only saying what his name means.

Christ. This name means "the anointed one." The Hebrew word *Messiah* means exactly the same. For a long time the Jewish people had looked for the Messiah, the deliverer who would set them free from their enemies and bring in a better day of righteousness and peace. When some of them called Jesus *Christ*, they meant that he was the Deliverer at last and was set apart to this task just as a ruler is anointed with oil. He was and is the Messiah, the Christ, the Deliverer. Christ was a spiritual leader who came not to establish an earthly realm like David's but to bring forth the realm of God on earth.

Son of God. Perhaps we can get close to the meaning of this name through some words Jesus himself spoke. Once, Philip said "Lord, show us the Father." Jesus answered, "Have I been with you all this time, Philip, and you still do not know me? He who has seen me has seen the Father" (John 14:8–9). How near he must have felt to God to be able to say that! Can you think of any other person who ever lived who would dare to say it? Jesus is as close to God as a child can be to parents, and as much like God as a child can be like his or her parent. All through the years Christians have called him "Son of God." To say it another way, in Jesus, God walked the earth as in no other person.

Teacher. Jesus was the teacher and the twelve disciples were his pupils. (*Disciples* means "pupil.") When we become his followers, he becomes our teacher, that we may learn how to live as participants in the realm of God.

Lord. This was the word that Greek-speaking people generally used when they wanted to say *God.* So you can see what the early Christians meant when they called Jesus *Lord.* They were lifting him up on a level with God.

What Jesus Has Meant to Some of His Followers

The names we have been thinking about show partly what Jesus has meant to Christians. For about two thousand years the pages of Christian history have been full of tributes to him. These tributes are found in many places.

In the Bible. We cannot begin to mention them all. One of the finest is found in Philippians 2:5–11. It was written by Paul.

In Christian literature. Here, too, there are many tributes to Jesus. In prose, we read such tributes as this one by Georgia Harkness:

> In Jesus . . . we see God [manifested] . . . in a human life. Jesus' name for God was Father, and uniquely beyond all other [persons] he lived as . . . [a child] of God ought to live. In Jesus we have the world's supreme revelation of God. Jesus lived like God; prayed to God; triumphed over temptation and pain in Godlike mastery; gave himself like God in love and suffering.[1]

Poets have written much about what Jesus meant to them, and they have helped others to express their own thoughts. For instance, the following poem, "Simon the Cyrenian Speaks," by Countee Cullen, expresses Cullen's thoughts:

> *He never spoke a word to me,*
> *and yet He called my name;*
> *He never gave a sign to me,*
> *and yet I knew and came.*
> *At first I said, "I will not bear*
> *His cross upon my back;*
> *He only seeks to place it there*
> *Because my skin is black."*
> *But He was dying for a dream,*
> *And He was very meek.*

And in His eyes there shone a gleam
[People] journey far to seek.
It was Himself my pity bought;
I did for Christ alone
What all of Rome could not have wrought
With bruise of lash or stone.[2]

One of the most beautiful hymns is "Beautiful Savior" (also known as "Fairest Lord Jesus.") Read it in your hymnal and notice how the thought runs in the second and third stanzas. There are many things that are beautiful in the earth below and in the heavens above—meadows, woodlands, sun-shine, moonlight, twinkling stars, angels—but Jesus is brighter and purer than all of them. This hymn is well worth committing to memory.

What Jesus Can Mean to Us

It is hard to put this in a few words, but we can try.

Through Jesus we can find the way to live. Jesus has already shown us how we should live. There is no excuse for our not knowing what the way is. He has gone before us in that way. He says to us, as he said to his disciples again and again, "Follow me."

Through Jesus we can find God. We can find God revealed in other places, of course. God is revealed in the beauties of tree and flower and sky and sea. God is revealed in the great prophets of the Old Testament and in other religious leaders both before and after Jesus. But nowhere is God to be found revealed so clearly as in the life, the death, the resurrection, the teachings, and the person of Jesus. When we want to know what God is like, we who are Christians turn to Jesus. First we ask ourselves, "What was Jesus like?" Then we are moved to say, "God is like that."

Through Jesus Christ we can be saved from "aimlessness and sin." There are two ways in which this is true:

1. Jesus saves us from our sins and gives us a purpose for our lives. He points out to us a richer, fuller life and asks us to follow him in it. He shows us what we ought to be.

2. He also saves us by helping us to find God. Sometimes, when we are deep in wrongdoing, nothing will lift us out but to remember that someone still loves us and believes in us.

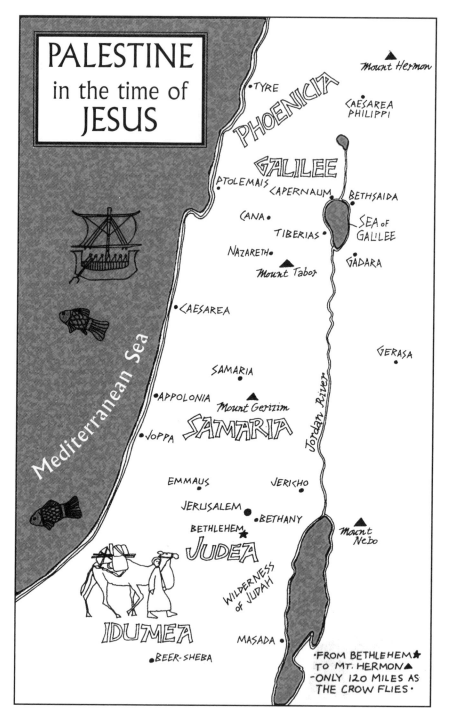

It can be a father, a mother, a teacher, a pastor, a friend. For countless people it has been God. Jesus shows us how much God loves us, even when we have done wrong. He shows us God's love through his teachings and his life, but most of all through his death on the cross. There we see how much he loved us. Since God is like him, that is the way God loves us all the time whether we deserve it or not, and that is the way God suffers when we sin. In the life and death of Jesus the love of God surrounds us and saves us from our sins. Year in and year out with just that sort of love God is trying to draw us to the way of life Jesus showed us.

One of the words that the Christian church has used to describe what we have been talking about is *atonement*. It really means "at-one-ment." When we have strayed away from God, and God and we have become two, then through Jesus we can be made one again.

This salvation is not just for this life. Because we believe that we live on after the death of our bodies, the new life Jesus gives us is endless. It is eternal life. "For God so loved the world that he gave his only Son, so that everyone who believes in him may have eternal life" (John 3:16).

Through Jesus the world can be saved from sin. This concept is explained in the words of the Statement of Faith of the United Church of Christ, which address God directly, "You judge people and nations by your righteous will declared through prophets and apostles . . . [and] in Jesus Christ . . . you have come to us, . . . reconciling the world to yourself." It is only when we follow Jesus' way of love and turn to serve God that wars and hatred and suffering will cease and the world will be reconciled to God and peoples to one another.

We have said that Jesus *can* mean all this to us. That is the right way to put it. None of this will happen automatically, but only as we come to know, love, and follow Jesus as Teacher, Lord, and Savior.

The Life of Jesus

Fill in the blanks with one or more words from the Scripture passages cited.

Jesus' family members were Jews. His mother's name was _Mary_.
and her husband's name was _Joespn_ (Matthew 1:16).
There were at least two girls and four boys besides Jesus. The boys' names
were _James_, _Joses_, _Jodas_, and _Simon_
(Mark 6:3).

Jesus was probably born in the year 6 B.C. in the town of _Bethlehem_
in the province of ___Judah___ (Matthew 2:1). His boyhood home was
the town of _Nazerath_ in the province of ___Gilalee___ (Luke 2:39).

The only fact we know about his boyhood is that he took a trip to
Jerqoalem (Luke 2:41) when he was ___12___ years old
(Luke 2:42).

Joseph was a _Carpenter_ (Matthew 13:55) by trade. We think that
Joseph died in Jesus' youth. So Jesus probably had to support the family by
his own hard toil for many years.

When Jesus was a man, a prophet named ___John___ (Mark 1:4) was
baptizing people to the south in the river _Jordan_ (Mark 1:5). Jesus
left the carpenter's bench and was baptized. He heard God's voice saying
to him, _your My Son_ (Mark 1:11).
This was the beginning of his short ministry of about two years. He was now
to give all his time to God's business.

First he went into the nearby _Wilderness_ (Mark 1:12), where he
spent ___40___ days (Mark 1:13) in what we call the temptation.
He was wrestling with the question of the best way of doing God's will in
bringing forth the realm of God.

For a few months he worked in the land of _Judean_ (John 3:22).

But soon John the Baptist was _arrested_ (Mark 1:14). It seemed
best for Jesus to return to his home province of _Gailalee_ (Mark 1:14).

There he spent most of his ministry. His headquarters were in the town
of _Capirnim_ (Mark 1:21) on the Sea of Galilee. Quite soon he called
two pairs of brothers to be his followers. Their names were: _Smon_
and _Andrew_ (Mark 1:16), _James_ and _John_
(Mark 1:19).

His ministry consisted first of teaching the great truths of God and the
realm of love and righteousness. Some of his finest teachings are gathered
together in Matthew 5–7. We call these teachings the Sermon on the Mount.
In 5:3–11 are nine verses called the Beatitudes. Each one begins with the
word _blessed_, which really means "happy." These verses tell who are the truly
happy people: the _poor_, those who _mourn_, the
meak, those who _hunger_, the _mercipul_, the
pure, and the _peacemaker_. In 5:44 he taught that we should
___love___ our enemies. In 6:9 he called God _Father_. In 6:25 he
taught that people should not worry about what they shall _eat_,

or _drink_, because God _provides_ (6:32). Rather, they should seek first _kingdom of god_ (6:33). In 7:24 he said that everyone who hears his sayings and follows them shall be like a _wise_ man who _built a house_

Luke has saved for us many beautiful parables, or stories, that Jesus told. One is about a good _Samaritan_ (10:33), and another is about a younger _son_ (15:13) who left his parents' home and wasted his inheritance and part of his life. Just as the father joyfully welcomed him back when he repented, so God welcomes us back into community when we are truly sorry and ask forgiveness for the wrongs we have done.

Jesus' ministry consisted of more than teaching. He also _cured_ (Mark 1:34) many sick people, who found in him new strength and hope.

At first he was quite popular. So many people flocked to follow him that _there was no room_ (Mark 2:2). Soon, however, opposition arose, particularly among the _Pharisees_ (Mark 2:6) and the _scribe_ (Mark 2:24). Among other things, they did not like it that he refused to be bound by their narrow laws about the _Sabbath_ (Mark 2:24).

Sometimes he took side trips, as for example across the Sea of Galilee into the country of the _Gerasenes_ (Mark 5:1).

Meanwhile he had gathered about him _12_ disciples (Mark 3:14). These he taught and then _sent out_ (Mark 6:7). When the opposition grew too strong he slipped away north into the neighborhood of _Tyre_ and _wwwwww_ (Mark 7:24).

Later he went north again, this time to _Saria Philippie_ (Mark 8:27). Here it was that Peter made his great statement of faith in Jesus, calling him for the first time _masian_ (Mark 8:29).

Jesus now saw the end of his life drawing near. He began to tell his disciples that _the son of man must suffer_ (Mark 8:31).

About this time he took his closest friends up on a high mountain, and he was _transfigured_ (Mark 9:2); that is, he looked different to them. It was a sort of second temptation. He wrestled with the problem of facing death, and he won. No wonder that he looked different. From now on he steadfastly set his face toward _Jerusalem_ (Luke 9:51), where he would be put to death.

He made his way there on the _cross Judea_ side (Mark 10:1) of the Jordan River. This, we think, was in the year A.D. 29, when Jesus was thirty-five years old.

At the beginning of the last week of his earthly life, he made a triumphal entry into Jerusalem, while those who followed shouted, "hosana to the son of david

"

(Matt 21:9). That night he spent in the nearby village of Bethany (Mark 11:11).

On Monday morning he went into the Temple in Jerusalem and Cleansed the temple

(Mark 11:15). On Tuesday and Wednesday he taught in Jerusalem, and probably spent some time quietly outside the city.

On Thursday evening he gathered his disciples together for a last supper in an Upper room (Mark 14:15). Here it was that he said that the bread and wine should remind his followers ever after of the sacrifice of his body and blood.

After the singing of a hymn they went outside the city to the Jerusalem (Mark 14:26). Here at a place called Mount of olives (Mark 14:32) he prayed in great earnestness to God. And here one of the twelve disciples, named Judas. (Mark 14:43), betrayed him into the hands of his enemies with a kiss.

Sometime that unhappy Thursday night or early Friday morning Jesus' captors led him to the high priest (Mark 14:53) to be questioned. As though Jesus did not have enough to bear, Peter, one of the inner circle of disciples, denied that he knew him (Mark 14:71).

Friday morning the religious leaders took him before the Roman governor, whose name was pilot (Mark 15:1), to be tried and—they hoped—sentenced to death. They charged him with claiming to be king of the Jews, which would not sound good to a Roman governor. After much maneuvering, Pilate, to satisfy the crowd, had Jesus whipped and ordered him to be crusfied (Mark 15:15).

The soldiers took him outside the city wall to a place called golgotha (Mark 15:22) and nailed him hand and foot to a wooden cross. This was about the 9 sour (Mark 15:25) hour (9 a.m. in our reckoning). While on the cross, Jesus spoke seven times. His words revealed his greatness. In the agony of the cross his first thoughts were for others, and only toward the end did he think of himself. These Seven Last Words from the Cross are as follows:

1. _Father forgive him_____
   _____ (Luke 23:34).

2. _____
   _____ (Luke 23:43).

3. _____
   _____ (John 19:26-27).

4. _____
   _____ (Mark 15:34).

5. _____
   _____ (John 19:28).

6. _____
   _____(John 19:30).

7. _____
   _____ (Luke 23:46).

Soon after the _3 pm_ (Mark 15:34) hour (3 p.m.) Jesus died. Two friends, _mary_ and _olemi_ (John19:38-39), buried Jesus in a rock-hewn tomb.

On Sunday morning three women named _____, _joesph_, and _nicademus_ (Mark 16:1) had their sorrow turned into joy by the glad assurance "_he's not here_" (Matthew 28:6). Their Lord was not dead. He was alive! They hurried to tell the good news to the _disciples_ (Matthew 28:8).

For forty days Jesus showed himself to many people, even to as many as _220_ at one time (1 Corinthians 15:6), and then people saw him no more. But Jesus Christ still lives. In the presence of God whom he served so well, he lives forevermore, and some day he will rule over all the earth.

The Names Jesus Called Himself

1. Matthew 8:20 _____

2. John 8:12 _____

3. John 10:7 _____

4. John 10:11 _____

5. John 11:25 _____

6. John 14:6 _____

7. John 15:1 _____

Passages that Show Jesus' Humanity

Luke 2:40 _____

Matthew 8:24 _____

John 19:28 _____

1 Corinthians 15:3 _____

Passages that Show His Divinity

Matthew 11:27 _____

Luke 4:43 _____

John 10:30 _____

John 12:49 _____

John 16:28 _____

Jesus' Purpose in Life

19:10 _____

_____

The Twelve Disciples

Write as many names as you can from memory. Then copy the rest from Mark 3:14–9.

Jesus' Appearances

To whom did Jesus appear after his resurrection?

Matthew 28:1–10 _____

Matthew 28:16–17 _____

Mark 16:9 _____

Luke 24:15–31 _____

John 20:19–24 _____

John 21:1–24 _____

John 20:26–28 _____

1 Corinthians 15:6–8 _____

Jesus' Character

List as many traits as you can that describe Jesus' character.

Passion Week

Write here the main happenings on each day of the last week of Jesus' life.

Sunday _____

_____(Mark 11:1–11)

Monday _____

_____(Matthew 21:12–13)

Tuesday _____

_____(Mark 12:28–34)

Wednesday _____

_____(Luke 22:1–6)

Thursday _____

_____(Matthew 26:17–29)

Friday _____

_____(Mark 15)

Saturday _____

_____(Matthew 27:62–66)

Sunday _____

_____(Mark 16:1–9)

Your Favorites

Write here in your own words your favorite story about Jesus.

Check your favorite parable of Jesus if it is listed here. If not, write in your favorite. Then write why the one you indicated is your favorite.

Matthew 7:24-27 _____

Matthew 25:14–30 _____

Mark 4:1–20 _____

Luke 10:25–37 _____

Luke 15:11–32 _____

Another _____

Why is it your favorite?

What Jesus Teaches Us to Do

Matthew 5:44 _____

Matthew 6:9a _____

Matthew 12:50 _____

Matthew 18:21–22 _____

Matthew 22:37–39 _____

Matthew 25:14–30 _____

Matthew 25:31–40 _____

Mark 1:15 _____

John 3:16 _____

John 15:12 _____

7

About the Holy Spirit

Jesus said, "God is spirit" and so we may say that there has always been a Holy Spirit. In the very beginning of the Bible we read that "the Spirit of God was moving over the face of the waters." In Job 33:4, Elihu says:

The spirit of God has made me,
and the breath of the Almighty gives me life.

Isaiah was conscious that God's Spirit was speaking and working through him. In Isaiah 48:16 the prophet says that "now the Lord God has sent me and God's Spirit."

All through the centuries some people have been conscious of God's Spirit working in them and through them, guiding their thoughts, giving them power to do great things for God. We often say that such people are inspired. The Latin word from which this English word comes means to "breathe into." In other words, God breathes the Spirit into these people and they become God-inspired, able to do and to say things that they were not able to do or to say by their own power.

At the time of Jesus' baptism, the Spirit of God came upon him and filled his whole being so that from that time on Jesus was able to live such a purposeful life and do such mighty works that people were conscious of an overwhelming power working through him.

When Jesus realized that he did not have long to live, he began to prepare his disciples for the time when he would no longer be with them in person. He promised them, "And I will ask the Father, and he will give you another Advocate to be with you for ever" (John 14:16), and he further explained, "But the Advocate, the Holy Spirit, whom the Father will send in my name, will teach you every thing, and remind you of all that I have said to you" (John 14:26). At another time he said, "But you will receive power when the Holy Spirit has come upon you; and you will be my witnesses in Jerusalem, and in all Judea and Samaria and to the ends of the earth" (Acts 1:8).

The Holy Spirit and the Christian Church

It was not until Pentecost that his followers understood what Jesus had meant. As they prayed behind locked doors they too were "filled with the Holy Spirit." Their mood was changed from one of defeat to one of victory. Their lives were changed through the power of the Holy Spirit working in them and through them, so that they were able to go out and do all the wonderful things about which we read in the New Testament.

But this giving of the Holy Spirit was not a one-time affair. As people joined the community of the followers of Jesus Christ they too "received the Holy Spirit." They too were conscious of God's Spirit leading them, teaching them, counseling them. In 1 Corinthians 2:9–13, Paul testified to the work of the Holy Spirit in the lives of Christians. Read this passage thoughtfully.

The Holy Spirit has been the guiding spirit of the Christian church down through the centuries. The Spirit is at work in the church today through many of its people—pastors, teachers, other youth, children, and adults—as they teach you what Jesus demands of his followers and as they help you to understand what is good and true.

When you promise to accept Christ as your Savior and Lord, he will become your Counselor and will guide you through life if you will listen to his voice. He will strengthen you and give you the power necessary to overcome difficulties and fears as you carry out the will of God in your life. He will comfort you in times of sorrow or trouble. Jesus said, "Lo, I am with you always," and he will be if you let the Holy Spirit lead you. Pray that you may be ready to receive the Spirit into your life and that you may be led by the Spirit from this day forward.

For Further Study

1. Reread what was said about the Holy Trinity on pages 32–33.

2. To understand the character and work of the Holy Spirit, study the Statement of Faith of the United Church of Christ (page 62–63) as well as hymns and answers to catechism questions that deal with the third Person in the Trinity.

What does the Statement of Faith say about the Holy Spirit?

In your hymnal, look in the topical index for hymns dealing with the Holy Spirit. Read these and notice what each poet has said about the Spirit. See also the Gloria Patri.

If you are using the Heidelberg Catechism, study questions 1, 21, and 53. What further information do you get about the Holy Spirit from the answers to these questions?

3. Read in Galatians 5:16–26 what Paul said is meant by living in the Spirit. What are the fruits of such living?

8

About Ourselves

What do you think of when you try to define or describe a human being? Here are some answers that have been given. Look them over and see if you think they are true.

A human being is a collection of chemicals, worth a few dollars. A human being is a highly evolved animal.

A human being is a spirit, part of God's Spirit.

A human being is a social being who likes to be with others.

A human being is the "temple of God."

A human being is a creative person who can express himself or herself through sounds that form words or beautiful music, through color and lines that make beautiful paintings or drawings, through scratches on paper that tell a story, and through inventions that make life easier and more meaningful.

A human being is a moral being who can tell right from wrong and can feel sorry for having done wrong.

A human being is eternal. He or she does not die when the body dies but lives on forever.

You may never have thought about this before, but it makes a great deal of difference how we think of ourselves. If we think of ourselves only as a collection of chemicals, what difference does it make what we do? But if we think of ourselves as the "temple of God," what we do makes a great deal of difference.

What Do We as Christians Believe About Ourselves?

We are children of God. Perhaps we have said this, or heard it said, so often that we have forgotten the wonder of it. We ought to repeat over and over to ourselves the words of 1 John 3:1: "See what love the Father has given us, that we should be called children of God."

If we are God's children, then we are somewhat like God. Children generally resemble their parents. It is not that our bodies look like God, but that our spirits resemble God's. God is keenly aware of the difference between right and wrong, and so are we—to some extent. God is interested in righteousness and goodness, and so are we—to some extent.

If we are God's children, we are precious. Any parent worthy of the name cares for each child. God is interested in what happens to each one of us. The Bible indicates that God wants the best for all people.

Everyone everywhere is a child of God. If we are God's children, we must believe that all are God's children. It is not the color of our skin or eyes that makes us children of God; nor the amount of money we have; nor the church we belong to; nor the country we live in. It is God's love for us as human beings.

We often sin. The Evangelical Catechism states that "no [one] has ever perfectly kept the law of God. By nature we are inclined to evil and have in many ways disobeyed God's commandments." Even though we are God's children, we often do things contrary to God's will—and that is what sin is.

Sometimes we take too narrow a view of what sin is. Sinful people, we say, are those who get drunk, or steal, or lie, or kill. Those are sinful acts, but Jesus found much sin among the "good" people of his time. The truth is that sin is broader than stealing and lying, and all of us sin at one time or another.

You remember that in the Garden of Gethsemane our Lord said, "Not my will, but yours, be done" (Luke 22:42). Sin is just the opposite of that. It is saying, "Not your will, but mine, be done." Sin is putting what we want ahead of what God wants. God wants only good for all people. We want something for ourselves and go after it regardless of what happens to other people. God wants the good of our souls. We want pleasure for our bodies and go after it regardless of what happens to our souls. Sin is following our own selfish wills instead of trying to follow God's will. That is why sin shuts us up in ourselves, cutting us off from other people and from God.

About Ourselves

We need God's forgiveness. When we have done what is wrong, we do not feel right inside until we have sought and found God's forgiveness and sometimes the forgiveness of the people we have wronged, as well. The parable of the lost son (Luke 15:11–32) teaches about our need of God's forgiveness and God's willingness to forgive. In this story the father stands for God. The younger son (the lost one) stands for all of us who stray so far from God's home that we are "lost." The older son stands for all of us who think we are doing our duty to God and yet cannot forgive someone who has strayed away. Such a person needs God's forgiveness too.

Notice what Jesus is saying in this parable.

The father is waiting for his son to come back, watching anxiously for him. So God is anxious and eager for us to come back when we have sinned.

The father cannot make the son come back. Neither can God make us come back.

The son is made to turn back home partly by the unhappiness that came to him when he was separated from his family, and partly by the remembrance of his father's goodness. So we are made to turn away from sin partly by the fact that sin doesn't pay, and partly by the thought of God watching for us to return.

When the son comes back home, he immediately confesses his sin, and because he is so evidently sorry, his father forgives him gladly. So God forgives us gladly when we confess our sins and come to God in true repentance, asking God to forgive us.

But the father could not forgive the son until the son "came to himself" and started back home. Neither can God forgive us until we recognize our sinfulness and seek God's forgiveness.

When the "good" son refuses to come in and join in the joy of the return of the wayward brother, the father comes out to him and pleads with him to see his point of view. So God seeks us out and pleads with us not to shut ourselves out of community with God and with our sisters and brothers. If we do, then we too need to seek the forgiveness of God and of our sisters and brothers.

The Christian church believes that it is through Christ that we are saved from our sins. Through faith in Jesus we can turn our backs on the old life and begin anew, knowing that our relationship with God has been restored (read John 3:16–17).

We find true happiness only by losing ourselves in something good. Here is a strange thought. We cannot be happy by trying to be happy. If we look for happiness in eating and drinking, all we find in the end is restlessness and wanting more of the same. But if we forget ourselves and become interested in other people, the work of the church, or some good cause like helping various racial and cultural groups to understand each other and to get along well together—we can find satisfaction! As Jesus put it: "Those who find their life will lose it, and those who lose their life for my sake will find it" (Matthew 10:39). This is one of the strangest facts about human beings. It must be that God has made us this way.

We are meant to live forever. This is an important part of our belief about ourselves. We do not understand altogether how we can live on after our bodies die. Neither can we picture very clearly just what the life beyond this one is like. But it is not necessary to know all about these matters. We only need to be sure that God is like a parent or guardian who cares for each one of us. If this is so, that care for us will not last for just seventy years, more or less; that caring will continue forever. The love of God is not limited to this life on this little planet we call the earth. Divine love goes everywhere. Therefore, we can face death for others or for ourselves, knowing full well it cannot separate us from God's love.

Some Questions to Think About

1.   In war, military leaders must sometimes calculate how many lives it will cost to capture a certain place or position. If it will take 100,000 lives, the attempt may not be made. If it will take 50,000, it may be worth it, they say. Does this fit the Christian belief that all human beings are children of God?
2.   We have said that all people are children of God. Does this mean that we should never go to war because the "enemy" is made up of children of God just as we are?

Does it mean that people of different races in America should have the exact same schools, equally good schools, or schools that offer only as much education as is needed and desired?

Does it mean that the people of India should have as high a standard of living as the American people (as much money, as good an opportunity to purchase a home, as many automobiles)?

Does it mean that a hardworking laborer in a factory should receive as much pay as the hardworking president of the firm, or one-half as much, or one-tenth as much, or one-hundredth as much?

3.   Why didn't God make us so that we could not sin?

4.   Why can't God forgive us until we want to be forgiven? When God forgives, does that wipe out the harm we have done? Does it guarantee that we will not sin again? What does God's forgiveness do to us?

5.   Who are the happiest people you know? Do they try to be happy? What is it that makes them happy?

6.   We believe that we are meant to live forever. Do you think God will give us a chance to grow and learn and do interesting and useful things after we die?

Draw Up a Class Statement of Belief

A good way of summarizing the last four chapters is for your class to prepare its own statement of belief. You might plan it in four parts, each beginning, "We believe . . ." and then describing the following:

1.   What you believe about God—character, forms of caring, actions.

2.   What you believe about Jesus Christ—who he is, what he is like, what he means to you.

3.   What you believe about the Holy Spirit.

4.   What you believe about yourselves and all people.

In each of these parts, use your own words as much as possible and write only what you really believe.

A Completion Test

Underscore the phrase that will complete the statement in light of our faith.

1.   All human beings are
    a. not children of God.
    b. children of God only if they are Christians.
    c. children of God.

2. We sin against God when we
   a. lie, steal, smoke, use drugs, and so forth.
   b. do things that are not according to God's will.
   c. follow the teachings of Jesus.

3. God will forgive us if we
   a. confess and repent of our sins.
   b. continue to seek our own desires.
   c. give a lot of money to the church.

4. We can best keep from sinning by
   a. putting our faith in Christ.
   b. keeping away from bad people.
   c. reading the Bible.

5. Jesus tells us that we can be happy if we will
   a. just do whatever we want to do.
   b. forget ourselves and work with him.
   c. work and get a lot of money and become successful.

6. Jesus teaches us to
   a. ask God for anything.
   b. ask God to give us what we need.
   c. say to God, "Not your will, but mine be done."

7. As human beings we have
   a. spirits like God's.
   b. bodies like God's.
   c. homes like God's.

8. It is wrong for us to show
   a. forgiveness to our friends.
   b. hatred toward those who hurt us.
   c. love toward our enemies.

9. God means for us to live
   a. only until our body dies.
   b. just so many planned years.
   c. forever.

9
What We Believe

Through all the centuries of Christianity—even today—people have tried to express their beliefs in writing. The most famous of these statements of belief are the Apostles' Creed and the Nicene Creed. Most such statements have begun with the words *I believe.* This was true back in the days when Latin was the common language. In Latin, *credo* means "I believe." And so we now call statements of belief *creeds.*

This chapter deals with creeds—the two historic ones just mentioned and the Statement of Faith of the United Church of Christ—with special emphasis on the Apostles' Creed.

Before looking at these creeds, take a look again at the statement of belief that your class has written. Then compare it with the ones that follow. What does your statement stress that these others do not? What do these others stress that yours does not mention? What points do they have in common?

The Apostles' Creed

I believe in God the Father Almighty, creator of heaven and earth.

I believe in Jesus Christ; God's only Son, our Lord, who was conceived by the Holy Spirit, born of the Virgin Mary, suffered under Pontius Pilate, was crucified, died, and was buried. He descended to the dead. On the third day he rose again; he ascended into heaven, he is seated at the right hand of the Father, and he will come to judge the living and the dead.

I believe in the Holy Spirit, the holy catholic church, the communion of saints, the forgiveness of sins, the resurrection of the body, and the life everlasting. Amen.

The Nicene Creed

We believe in one God, the Father, the Almighty, maker of heaven and earth, of all that is, seen and unseen.

We believe in one Lord, Jesus Christ, the only Son of God, eternally begotten of the Father, God from God, Light from Light, true God from true God, begotten, not made, of one being with the Father; through him all things were made. For us and for our salvation he came down from heaven, was incarnate of the Holy Spirit and the Virgin Mary and became truly human. For our sake he was crucified under Pontius Pilate; he suffered death and was buried. On the third day he rose again in accordance with the Scriptures; he ascended into heaven, and is seated at the right hand of the Father. He will come again in glory to judge the living and the dead, and his kingdom will have no end.

We believe in the Holy Spirit, the Lord, the giver of life, who proceeds from the Father and the Son; who with the Father and the Son is worshiped and glorified, who has spoken through the prophets. We believe in one holy catholic and apostolic church. We acknowledge one baptism for the forgiveness of sins. We look for the resurrection of the dead, and the life of the world to come. Amen.

The Statement of Faith of The United Church of Christ

We Believe in you, 0 God, Eternal Spirit, God of our Savior
 Jesus Christ and our God, and to your deeds we testify:
 You call the worlds into being
  create persons in your own image,
  and set before each one the ways of life and death.
 You seek in holy love to save all people from aimlessness and sin.
 You judge people and nations by your righteous will declared
  through prophets and apostles.
 In Jesus Christ, the man of Nazareth, our crucified and risen Savior,
  you have come to us
  and shared our common lot,
  conquering sin and death
  and reconciling the world to yourself.
 You bestow upon up your Holy Spirit,
  creating and renewing the church of Jesus Christ,
  binding in covenant faithful people of all ages, tongues, and races.

You call us into your church
>> *to accept the cost and joy of discipleship,*
>> *to be your servants in the service of others,*
>> *to proclaim the gospel to all the world and resist the powers of evil,*
>> *to share in Christ's baptism and eat at his table*
>> *to join him in his passion and victory.*
> *You promise to all who trust you*
>> *forgiveness of sins and fullness of grace,*
>> *courage in the struggle for justice and peace,*
>> *your presence in trial and rejoicing,*
>> *and eternal life in your realm which has no end.*
> *Blessing and honor, glory and power be unto you. Amen.*

How the Apostles' Creed Started

For many centuries Christians have stated their faith in the words of the Apostles' Creed. They are sacred with age. When and where and how were they first used?

The creed grew slowly over many years. It was not written by the twelve apostles. You cannot find it anywhere in the Bible. Of course, the ideas it contains are there, and the apostles believed these ideas with all their hearts. But the creed itself came later.

The only statement of belief that was asked of the very first Christians was that they assert that "Jesus Christ is Lord" (see Acts 16:31; Romans 10:9; 1 Corinthians 12:3; and Philippians 2:11).

The earliest form of the Apostles' Creed was probably drawn up about A.D. 150 at Rome. The language in which it first took shape was probably Greek. It was not so long then as it is now. A scholar who has studied the matter carefully thinks that this is the way it was written at the time:

> I believe in God the Father Almighty and in Christ Jesus his Son, who was born of Mary the Virgin, was crucified under Pontius Pilate and buried, on the third day rose from the dead, ascended into heaven, sitteth on the right hand of the Father, from whence he cometh to judge the living and dead; and in Holy Spirit, resurrection of flesh.[1]

And how was it used? It was part of the service of baptism, by which new members were taken into the church. It would be quite natural to ask new members to say publicly what they believed. To help them express their beliefs, this brief creed was taught to them, and they were asked to repeat it when they were baptized.

You will notice that the statement falls into three parts—a short part on God, a long one on Christ, and a short one again on the Holy Spirit. This division may have been suggested by Matthew 28:19: "Go therefore and make disciples of all nations, baptizing them in the name of the Father and of the Son and of the Holy Spirit." You can easily see that these words could be added to until they became the Apostles' Creed.

The earliest form of this creed was planned at almost every point to guard against the wrong ways of thinking that were current at that time. The man whose ideas seem to have been feared most was Marcion. Marcion had the strange belief that the God of the Jews and the God of the Christians were two different gods. The one was to be found in the Old Testament, and the other in the New Testament. The second was the parent of Jesus and was altogether good, but not almighty. This God did not make the world and did not rule the world. It was the Old Testament God who did these things. Therefore, to make sure that new Christians would not fall into such a wrong way of thinking, the Apostles' Creed was started with the statement "I believe in God the Father Almighty."

Marcion and some others could not bear to think that Jesus actually lived and suffered on this earth. They said he just seemed to. So the Apostles' Creed comes out boldly and says that Jesus was really born, crucified, and buried.

How the Apostles' Creed Grew to Its Present Form

The earliest form of the Apostles' Creed is only a part of our present one. Many familiar phrases are missing. These phrases were added little by little, as they were needed.

The phrase *the forgiveness of sins* was added shortly after A.D. 200. Everybody believed that baptism washed away all a person's sins up to that moment. But what about sins committed after baptism? Could they be forgiven? Some said they could not, but the main body of the church said they could. And so a phrase was added to the creed to make sure that new Christians would have the right belief on this point.

The phrase *holy church* was probably added about the same time. The word *catholic* was put in during the fourth century. It does not mean "Roman Catholic," but "universal." That is why some of our churches prefer the phrase the *One Holy Universal Christian Church.*

Descended into hell (or Hades) was added about the year 400. At that time hell was not considered a place of punishment; it was simply the place where the dead were thought to be.

And so it went. By the sixth century Christians in western Europe were repeating the creed exactly the way we do now (not in English, of course), and it has lived on ever since.

When you say the Apostles' Creed, then, either at your confirmation service or in an ordinary service, think back to all the people who have used these words in centuries past, and think about all the people who are using it now around the world.

Its Meaning for Us

When you say the Apostles' Creed, do you always think of and understand what you are saying? Without trying to explain every word, let us try to see what, in general, each part means so that the creed can help us to grow in the Christian life, as it has helped millions before us.

I believe in God the Father Almighty, Maker of heaven and earth. When we say these words, we mean that we believe in an unseen Spirit who is in and through and behind everything we see. God is all-powerful. God made everything there is in the heavens above and on the earth beneath. And—most wonderful of all!—God is our Parent. Since this is true, we need fear nothing in life or death, for this is God's world.

And in Jesus Christ, his only (begotten) Son, our Lord. We believe also in Jesus. We believe that he is the Christ, the anointed one set apart to do God's will. We believe that he is God's only Son. All of us are children of God, but he alone is so fully and completely God's Child that we can know what God is like by looking at him. This same Jesus is our Lord, whom we will follow and serve to the end.

Who was conceived by the Holy Spirit, born of the Virgin Mary. We believe that Jesus' life came both from God and from humans. It came from humans, because Mary his mother—for all her goodness—was a human being like any other. But it came also from God. It was so fine that it must have had its source in God.

Suffered under Pontius Pilate, was crucified, dead, and buried. We believe that Jesus' love for people and his obedience to God's will were so great that he could not stop short of the cross. So he suffered many things in body and in spirit under the Roman governor, Pontius Pilate. He hung in agony on the cross. He died and was laid to rest in a tomb.

He descended into hell (Hades). (See page 227 for an explanation of the terms hell and Hades.) We believe that Jesus' went even to the place of the dead, so that there is nothing in life or death that can separate us from God.

The third day he rose again from the dead. We believe that Jesus lives today and forevermore.

He ascended into heaven, and sitteth at the right hand of God the Father Almighty. We believe that throughout all the ages Jesus has the foremost place of honor and love in the presence of God whom he served so well.

From thence he shall come to judge the quick and the dead. We believe that all people, those now living and those who have died, will be judged by God in Christ.

I believe in the Holy Spirit. We believe that God's Spirit is even now at work in us and in the world to fulfill the divine plans for God's realm.

The holy catholic church (or the One Holy Universal Christian Church), the communion of saints. We believe in one great church extending throughout the world and through every age, made up of Christians of every denomination and race and nation. We believe that at the communion table, as well as during other times, we can feel near to them all, including those who are no longer present in this life.

The forgiveness of sins. We believe that God will gladly forgive our sins if we turn to God in all sincerity.

The resurrection of the body, and the life everlasting. We believe that even though we will die, we will live again. Read what Paul says about this subject in 1 Corinthians 15.

How the Nicene Creed Came to Be

Like the Apostles' Creed, the Nicene Creed also developed as the years went on. It, too, grew out of the need in the early church for a confession of faith in connection with baptism. It was developed especially for the Eastern churches, whereas the Apostles' Creed was more for the Western churches.

The original Nicene Creed dates from the first ecumenical council of the Christian church, which met at Nicea in Asia Minor in the year 325. The creed developed there was much shorter than the one quoted earlier, which is the one used in all Greek and Russian Orthodox churches and also in the Roman, Anglican, and Lutheran churches. In the Reformed churches, the Nicene Creed is used less often because its language is more abstract than the biblical language of the Apostle's Creed.

How the United Church of Christ Statement of Faith Came to Be

During the process of merging the Evangelical and Reformed church and the Congregational Christian churches into the United Church of Christ, a committee was appointed to draw up a statement of faith for the new church—one growing out of our own times and written in our present-day language. The committee worked long and prayerfully, and it finally presented a draft to the Second General Synod of the United Church of Christ held at Oberlin, Ohio, July 5–9, 1959. This was approved with a few changes and appears on pages 60–61 in a "doxological" version addressed to God. The General Synod recommends that it be used in congregational worship, in private devotions, and in study. In line with this recommendation, your confirmation class might study the statement much as you did the Apostles' Creed—thought by thought.

Some Questions to Consider

1.   Why, do you suppose, did the early Christians devote so much of their statements of belief to Jesus Christ?

2.   Why did they say nothing about the greater part of his life but go straight from his birth to his crucifixion?

3.   If you could keep only one part of the Apostles' Creed or the Nicene Creed, which part would you keep? Why?

4.   What is the biggest difference you see between the two ancient creeds and the Statement of Faith of the United Church of Christ?

5.   Is there value in using various statements of belief in worship services? If so, why? If not, why not?

Some Things to Do

1.   If you are using a catechism, see how it explains the various parts of the Apostles' Creed. (If you are using the Evangelical Catechism, read questions 12–15, 59–71, and 75–99. If you are using the Heidelberg Catechism, see questions 24–58.)

2.   Talk to several adult Christians and ask each one what the saying of a creed means to them.

3.   Study the creed used most frequently in your church. Compare it with others. Find out why it was selected as the one to be used in your church.

Test on the Creeds

1.   What does the word *creed* mean? Is it different from a statement of faith? If so, explain.

2.   The Apostles' Creed and Nicene Creed tell what Christians have believed about the following:

a. _____

b. _____

c. _____

d. _____

e. _____

f. _____

g. _____

h. _____

3. What is the difference between a creed and a prayer?

A prayer is _____

A creed is _____

4. What do the first paragraphs of the Apostles' and Nicene creeds tell us about God? That God is:

a. _____

b. _____

c. _____

5. What does the second paragraph of the Apostles' Creed say about Christ? That he is:

a. _____

b. _____

c. _____

d. _____

e. _____

f. _____

g. _____

h. _____

6. What does the Nicene Creed say about the Holy Spirit?
To what "deeds" of God do we testify in the United Church Statement of Faith?

Your Beliefs

1. Do you believe that God is present in life today? _____
    Explain your answer.

2. How does God work in the world today?

3. Why do you call Jesus *Lord*?

4. In what ways does the Holy Spirit work in your life?

5. How do you know that the Holy Spirit is with you?

6. To be forgiven of your sins, what must you do first?

7. What do you believe about eternal life?

PART THREE
The Christian Way of Life

10

Christians Trust In God

We now begin four chapters on the Christian way of life. The Christian way of life means trust in God, caring for others, disciplining ourselves, and seeking the realm of God.

How far we fall short of this way of life! We do not trust and love God with all our hearts. Instead, we worry and fret over little things as though there were no God to trust. Sometimes we actually go along day after day without thinking about God at all. Neither do we love other people to the point of suffering for them as Jesus did. Instead, we are selfish and self-centered a good part of the time.

Even if we try all our lives, we will still fall short. But we must try nevertheless, and keep on trying. With God's help, we can make some headway. Paul was speaking for us all when he wrote to the Philippians (3:13–14): "Beloved, I do not consider that I have made it my own; but this one thing I do: forgetting what lies behind and straining forward to what lies ahead, I press on toward the goal for the prize of the heavenly call of God in Christ Jesus."

How Did Jesus Trust in God?

To Jesus, God was more real than anything else—more real than the Sea of Galilee or the hills around Jerusalem, more real than Peter or even his mother, Mary. Jesus trusted God absolutely. He loved God. He did God's will. He lived in God's presence constantly. All this is seen time and again in his life.

The following passages tell, in Jesus' own words, how he lived with God. They run from the time he was a boy of twelve until his death. As you write the main thought of each verse, try to picture Jesus when he said it, and try to imagine how he felt toward God at the time.

Luke 2:49 _____

_____

Matthew 6:30 _____

_____

Matthew 11:27 _____

_____

Matthew 22:37 _____

_____

John 5:17 _____

_____

Matthew 26:39 _____

_____

Luke 23:46 _____

_____

We Too Should Trust in God

God is our Parent. God cares for us. God is alive and at work in the world today, just as when Jesus walked the earth. As Christians we are to trust, obey, love, and worship God. This is the Christian way of life.

It is easy to trust in God when we are well, the sun is shining, the world is at peace, and everybody is happy. But in the hard times of life it is not always easy. In each of the following instances, what would it mean truly to trust in God?

1. A girl came to her church school teacher at a time when thousands of people were being put out of work because of a poor economy. She complained bitterly that her father had lost his job and had not been able to find another. She said that her father was a good man, a faithful member of the church. She herself had prayed and prayed that God would find a job for him, but nothing had happened. If you had been her teacher, what would you have told this girl? Should she trust God to find a job for her father without her father's help? Should she encourage her father to trust in God's care and to train himself for another type of work? Should she be told that God is always trying to provide for all God's children, and it is not God's fault, but people's, that her father is out of work? Should she be taught to trust God to care for the members of her family, even though some of them might go hungry?

2. In the war in Vietnam thousands of civilians lost their lives, including men, women, and children. Terrible things happen in war. Sometimes it looks as though there is no God in whom we can trust. What does it mean to trust in God when the world seems to be falling to pieces? Does it mean that we can sit quietly by and wait for God to set things right? Does it mean that if we pray earnestly enough, God will grant victory to our side? Because war is caused by people, God has nothing to do with starting it or stopping it. Does that mean that God is surely suffering with God's children?

3. Hillary is trying to decide what vocation to follow. She is about to enter senior high school and must make up her mind soon so that she can choose the right courses. Can she trust God to give her an exact answer if she prays earnestly about it? Or should she believe rather that God has given her a good mind and wise friends, and that God expects her to secure guidance through these? Or is there some other way in which Hillary can show her trust?

4. The members of a church school class were talking about being saved. Dillon was of the opinion that we do not need to trust in God for help, that we can save ourselves by doing the right and avoiding the wrong. Robin did not agree. She said that of course we should try our level best to do what's right, but sometimes we fail so badly that only a firm trust in God's unchanging love can do us any good. Who do you think was right? The answer to question 80 in the Evangelical Catechism—"Faith is complete trust in God and willing acceptance of [God's] grace in Jesus Christ"—is worth studying and memorizing in this connection. (If you don't understand the concept of grace, see page 227.)

Jesus kept his trust in God unbroken, even during the hardest times. So did Paul. His life was filled with persecutions and hardships, but through it all he could write: "For I am convinced that neither death, nor life, nor angels, nor rulers, nor things present, nor things to come, nor powers, nor height, nor depth, nor anything else in all creation, will be able to separate us from the love of God in Christ Jesus our Lord" (Romans 8:38–39). (It might be helpful to commit these grand words to memory and carry them with you so long as you live.)

Showing Our Trust in God Through Prayer

One of the chief ways of showing our trust in God and of making that trust still deeper is prayer. When we truly pray, we are truly living in God's presence. Prayer is not mainly asking God for something. We often think it is, but we should know better from Jesus' example in the Garden of Gethsemane. In the midst of great agony of soul, this was his prayer: "My Father, if it is possible, let this cup pass from me, yet, not what I want, but what you want" (Matthew 26:39). In this prayer, Jesus was striving to know God's will and to do it. So prayer is not so much asking God to do something for us, as asking ourselves to do something for God.

One of the early leaders of the church, Clement of Alexandria, has given us an illustration to help us think about prayer in the right way. He said that when sailors in a ship pull on a rope fastened to an anchor, they do not pull the anchor toward them, but themselves toward the anchor. In the same way, when we pray, our words should not so much pull God toward us but pull us toward God.

Someone else has said that prayer is a time exposure of the soul to God. In a time exposure the shutter of the camera is opened and held open steadily until the image is imprinted on the film. In the same way, in prayer we open our souls to God, thinking about God and God's will, until something of God's image is imprinted on our lives.

When Jesus prayed in Gethsemane his soul was exposed to God until the image of God's goodness was stamped on it perfectly. When he rose to his feet and went out to be crucified, God's will was his will. God's goodness was his goodness. God's love was his love. The image of God was stamped on his soul.

Our Prayer Life

A good part of our praying, then, ought to consist of the following:

    1. Thanks to God for all God has done for us.

    2. A request for knowledge and strength to do something for God.

    3. Silent waiting for God's direction.

These steps might well serve as an outline for our individual devotions. *First,* we could praise God for food, clothing, friends, beauty all around us, Jesus Christ, the church, and God's never-failing love in which we put our trust no matter what the future may bring. *Second,* we could seek earnestly for God's will for our lives at home, at school, at play, and at work. We could also pray for strength to do God's will. The words we say are not so important as what we think and feel about God. *Third,* we could hold ourselves open to God's direction. We could make a time exposure of our souls to God.

Do you make a practice of daily devotions, either morning or evening, or both? Do you feel that it is worthwhile to do so? How long should such a period be? What should it include?

Many young people, as well as some older people, have found much help in *These Days* and *Upper Room*—books containing a page of devotional suggestions for each day in the year. Have you tried using these books? If so, have you found them helpful? If not, do you think guides of this sort might be helpful?

The Lord's Prayer

This prayer is so called because our Lord himself gave it to us. This makes it very precious—more precious than any other. You can find it in Matthew 6:9–13, and a shorter form in Luke 11:2–4. Compare the prayer as given in the Bible and the way you are used to saying it. What differences do you find?

Doubtless we understand the Lord's Prayer fairly well. Nevertheless, it may mean even more to us if we make a special study of it. Notice first of all how it is made up. It has the following parts:

1. The *address,* naming the One to whom we pray	Our Father in heaven,
2. *Petitions* or requests centering in God	hallowed be your name, your kingdom come, your will be done, on earth as in heaven.
3. *Petitions* or requests centering in ourselves	Give us today our daily bread, Forgive us our sins as we forgive those who sin against us. Save us from the time of trial and deliver us from the evil.
4. A *conclusion* of praise to God	For the kingdom, the power, and the glory are yours, now and for ever. Amen.

A few of the words and phrases need some explanation.

The phrase *Hallowed be thy name* means "May your name be made holy (or kept sacred)."

Bread stands for our bodily needs.

But why is the next phrase, *as we forgive those who sin against us* added? This means that we are not fit to be forgiven unless we forgive others. We are not big enough. We are not loving enough. We are not unselfish enough.

One thing very important about the prayer as a whole is that it never speaks of *me* or *mine*. It is always us and our. When we pray the Lord's Prayer, we do not come to God alone. We take with us all God's children everywhere.

If you are using a catechism, see questions 103–111 in the Evangelical Catechism and questions 120–129 in the Heidelberg Catechism for further information on the various parts of the Lord's Prayer.

The Lord's Prayer is the finest prayer we know. It is worth understanding. We should always say it reverently and give careful thought to the meaning of all the words.

Questions on Prayer

1. What is prayer?

2. Why do we pray?

3. In what ways does God answer our prayers?

4. Most prayers consist of two parts. What are they?
    a.
    b.

5. Write a brief prayer in your own words, using the Lord's Prayer as a guide.

The Prayers of Jesus

The Bible tells of many times when Jesus prayed, and sometimes even gives his very words. Look up the following prayers of Jesus and indicate with a few words the kind of prayer each is (thanks, personal commitment, prayer for others, and so on):

Matthew 6:9–13 _____

Matthew 11:25–26 _____

Luke 22:42 _____

Luke 23:34 _____

Luke 23:46 _____

John 11:41 _____

John 12:27–28 _____

John 17 _____

Questions on the Lord's Prayer

1. From whom does the Lord's Prayer come? _____

2. For what do we pray in this prayer? _____

3. In whom do the first three petitions center? _____

4. In whom do the last four petitions center? _____

5. What does the word *debts* mean in this prayer? _____

6. Where in the Bible is the Lord's Prayer? _____

7. Why do we add the conclusion of praise to God to the prayer as it appears in the Bible? _____

11

Christians Care for Others

In the last chapter we focused on how we as Christians should live in relation to God. In this chapter we will look at how we should live in relation to others. Between these two, as it were, we stop and remind ourselves that the Old Testament contains a list of our duties to God and people that has been guiding Jews and Christians for many hundreds of years. It is the Ten Commandments. These come down to us from a time long before Jesus lived. Probably, to begin with, some of them were shorter than they now are. The fact that there were ten of them made them easier to remember—one for each finger of the two hands. Taking only the key phrase of each, we have the following:

	1.	You should have no other gods before me.
	2.	You shall not make yourself an idol. You shall not
Duties		bow down to them and worship them.
to God	3.	You shall not make wrongful use of the name
		of the Lord your God.
	4.	Remember the Sabbath day and keep it holy.
	5.	Honor your father and your mother.
	6.	You shall not murder.
Duties	7.	You shall not commit adultery.
to Others	8.	You shall not steal.
	9.	You shall not bear false witness against your neighbor.
	10.	You shall not covet.

When we arrange the key thoughts in this way, it is easy to see that they fall into two groups of four and six each. It is also easy to see how our Lord could sum them up in love to God and love to our neighbors (Matthew 22:37–40). Every Christian should commit the Ten Commandments to memory. You will find them in Exodus 20:2–17. (A slightly different wording is given in Deuteronomy 5:6–21.)

A few of the words and phrases may not be quite clear.

To *make wrongful use of the name of God* means to use it lightly, jokingly, irreverently. This we should never do.

The seventh commandment tells us that the deepest love between men and women must be kept for husband and wife and never given to another.

To *bear false witness against a neighbor* means to say something untrue about anyone.

The tenth commandment is somewhat like the eighth but goes far beyond it. *Covet* means "want." So this commandment means that we must not even want something that belongs to another person; we must not even want to steal.

If you are using a catechism, see questions 33–51 in the Evangelical Catechism or questions 91–113 in the Heidelberg Catechism for a more detailed study of each commandment.

Look up what the *Interpreter's Bible,* volume 1 or the *New Interpreter's Bible,* volume 1, says about the Decalogue (another name for the Ten Commandments). Your church library may have some books on the Ten Commandments that can help you explore the deeper meaning behind the words.

Jesus believed in knowing and obeying the Ten Commandments (see Matthew 19:16–19), but he also gave a deeper meaning to many of them (see Matthew 5:21–37). So every Christian should know these ancient laws and keep them in the spirit of Jesus.

How Did Jesus Care for Others?

Jesus cared for everyone. There were no exceptions. He saw in every person a child of the heavenly Parent, and his own sister or brother. It is amazing to go through the Gospels and see the different kinds of people whom he helped or to whom he was friendly. He cared for the Samaritans, whom the Jews despised as foreigners and half-breeds. He cared for the tax collectors (publicans), whom everybody disliked. He cared for lepers, full of ugly sores, and for insane people (those who had "demons"). He cared for his worst enemies. This will mean more to you if you will see for yourself a few instances of Jesus' great love for all people.

To whom was Jesus showing friendship in

Mark 10:17–21? _____

Luke 7:12–13? _____

Luke 7:37–48? _____

Luke 8:35? _____

Luke 18:15–16? _____

Luke 19:2–6? _____

Luke 23:34? _____

John 19:26–27? _____

How *much* did Jesus care for all people? The answer is in John 15:13: "No one has greater love than this, to lay down one's life for one's friends." This our Lord did. More than this no one can do.

We Too Should Care for Others

The Christian way of life is to care for others as Jesus did. Our Lord has left us in no doubt on this point. He has given us a new commandment—not ten, but one—and it is this: "A new commandment I give to you, that you love one another; even as I have loved you, that you also love one another. By this everyone will know that you are my disciples, if you have love for one another" (John 13:34–35). Ever since, the followers of Jesus have been trying to care for others as he did. Let us look briefly at the lives of several of these true followers.

Theirs Is the Christian Way of Life

1. *Martin Luther King, Jr.,* was born in Atlanta, Georgia, January 15, 1929. His decision to become a minister came after many hours of prayerful thought; he had once wanted to become a lawyer or doctor. However, being born into a family of preachers, becoming a minister was almost inevitable.

In 1954, at the age of twenty-six, Dr. King was called to be the pastor of the Dexter Avenue Baptist Church in Montgomery, Alabama. Alabama, at that time, was a very segregated state. A few months after moving to Montgomery, an African American woman named Rosa Parks refused to give up her seat on a bus to a white man, as the law required. This historic event prompted the Montgomery Bus Boycott. This boycott was extremely effective—African Americans were eventually allowed to sit in any seat they wanted on Montgomery buses.

As a new clergy person, Dr. King was asked to join a committee, the Montgomery Improvement Association. This association was responsible for planning future boycotts. By surprise, Dr. King was chosen by his peers to become the president of the Montgomery Improvement Association. He did not want this position because he was quite young and new to the city. He reluctantly accepted and realized he was faced with an even bigger surprise. Within one hour of being elected, he had to make a speech about future boycotts!

Dr. King faced over four thousand people in a crowded church. The speech he gave that day would begin his fight for civil rights. Little did he know that this would be the beginning of the civil rights movement in the United States, which would eventually change the world.

2. *Albert Schweitzer* was born on a strip of land on the border between France and Germany. His birth year was 1875. From childhood he could not bear to see any living thing suffer. For example, he would not shoot birds with a slingshot, as other boys did. Neither could he be comfortable when he saw people all around him who were unhappy. As a youth he made up his mind to continue his studies and his music until he was thirty; then he would go to some place where people needed him, and he would serve them the rest of his life. He was blessed with abilities such as few people have. He became the president of a theological seminary, the author of books known around the world, a great pipe-organist, and a student of pipe organ building—all of this before he was thirty years old.

In 1905 he decided to study medicine and go as a medical missionary to

Africa. The people there needed him. In 1913 he arrived at Lambarene, where he was to be the doctor. Patients came to him suffering from tropical diseases or from great open sores. His equipment was scanty. For a while he had to work in a made-over chicken house. To keep his spirits up, he played his beloved piano. When through medicine or through an operation he succeeded in putting a stop to pain, he would tell the patient about Jesus, in whose name he had come to Africa.

During World War I, because he was a German, he was taken to France as a prisoner. When the war was over, he went back to Africa to continue to care for others. This is the Christian way of life.

3.   There was a time when no self-respecting English woman would be a nurse. Sick people had to endure untold suffering without a nurse's help, or at least without a trained nurse's help. This was bad enough in peacetime, but it was worse during war. The person who changed this situation was *Florence Nightingale.* She was born in 1820 of a wealthy English family. As she grew to womanhood she could not shut out of her thoughts the sufferings of the sick. When she was seventeen, Florence nursed her neighbors through a siege of influenza. That same winter she felt definitely called by God to a life of service to the sick. In due time she became head of a nursing home.

Then came the Crimean War. There was no Red Cross. There were no women nurses for the English wounded. Florence went to the Black Sea, along with others. She found row after row of beds with wounded and dying soldiers, actually stretching for several miles. Everything was dirty. There was no soap. There was not even a broom. The food was poor. Few of the men had knives or forks to eat with. Florence set to work with courage and energy, and she brought some comfort to these patient soldiers. They called her the Good Lady. Queen Victoria sent her a piece of jewelry with the words "Blessed are the merciful." After the war Florence continued her work of training nurses who would care for the sick. This, also, is the Christian way of life.

4.   *Mother Teresa of Calcutta,* better known as Mother Teresa was born in 1910. In 1928 Mother Teresa went to India where she joined the Sisters of Loretto. She became a teacher and later the principal of a convent school there. Responding to the call to minister to the poor, Mother Teresa left the convent to work alone in the slums of Calcutta.

The need of poor people was so great that she went to Paris for medical training before opening her first school for destitute children. In 1952 she opened her House for the Dying. Mother Teresa's courage and desire to do

God's work on earth moved her in 1957 to work with lepers. She has always been willing to work with the least, the lost, and the left out. In 1971 she was awarded the Pope John XXIII Peace Prize. She received the Nobel Peace Prize in 1979.

What Can We Do?

Jesus has told us plainly what we can do. To begin with, we can follow the Golden Rule in our dealings with everyone about us. You will find this rule in Matthew 7:12.

How would you like to be treated
- if you were physically challenged and lived in a community without handicap accessible facilities?
- if you were a parent or guardian who lost your job and were unable to pay your bills and care for your family?
- if you were a younger brother or sister who felt neglected?
- if you were a Jew in a community made up mostly of non Jews?
- if you were a person of color in a community where white people held the positions of influence?
- if you had been lying sick in bed for the past month?
- if you were a prisoner in a jail cell?

The first step in caring for other people is to try to put ourselves in their places, to see life as they see it, and to try to treat them as we would want to be treated.

Jesus also said that we are to treat people as the good Samaritan did (see Luke 10:25-37). We must show mercy and give help to anyone anywhere who is in need. Is there anything that you could do as individuals or as a class to follow Jesus' teaching and example?

Will your congregation be collecting an offering soon for a children's home, a home for the elderly, a hospital, a mission station, or a relief fund of any sort? If so, what part could you take in it?

Does your community sponsor any fund drives, such as a walk against hunger or AIDS? If so, what part could you take in it?

Are there any families in your congregation or community who are in need? If so, what could you do to help?

Are there any sick or shut-in members of your church who would appreciate a visit regularly? Could you read the Bible to them? Sing some hymns for them? Could you take them a copy of your church bulletin or the *United Church News*? or some flowers?

Is there a children's ward in a hospital nearby? Do the children have toys, pictures, and scrapbooks enough to make the time go a little faster? Could you supply some? Check with the hospital.

Are there any new families in your community who you could help welcome? Could you invite them to your church? What could you do for them and with them at school?

The Ten Commandments and You

Write in the blanks what each of the commandments means to you. Put all your statements in a positive form (what you should do if you keep the commandments). Make the statements brief.

1. _____

2. _____

3. _____

4. _____

5. _____

6. _____

7. _____

8. _____

9. _____

10. _____

A Quiz on the Ten Commandments

1. Where in the Bible are the Ten Commandments? _____

     _____

2. Into how many groups may the Ten Commandments be divided? What

     are they? _____

     _____

3. What is meant by the Sabbath day? _____

     _____

4. What day do most Christians think of when they say the fourth

     commandment? _____ Why do they? _____

     _____

     _____

5. What two Old Testament verses did Jesus use to summarize the Ten

     Commandments?

     a. Deuteronomy 6:5 _____

     _____

     _____

     b. Leviticus 19:18 _____

     _____

6. What additional commandment did Jesus give? (John 13:34)

     _____

     _____

     _____

12

Christians Care for Themselves

Let's try to envision Jesus as he stood on trial before Pontius Pilate, the Roman governor. The courtroom was full of spectators. There were Roman soldiers who stood watch and others who wanted to see the outcome. Jesus was on trial for his life and Pontius Pilate held the power of life and death over him, or so it seemed.

How would you describe Jesus' thoughts and feelings at this moment? Do you think that he was frightened?

Do you think Jesus was trying to decide on a plan of action to save himself?

Do you think Jesus was in control of himself in such a situation of grave danger?

It is only rarely that we meet such a danger. Our own self-control must usually be shown in quite ordinary situations. Nevertheless, our self-control involves the stewardship of everything God has given us—our body, our money, our time, our life.

Care for Your Body

A speaker once said: "I am not my body. I am more than my body. I can boss my body. I can tell it to go this way, and it goes." (Here he walked across the platform to the right.) "Then I can tell it to go the other way, and it goes." (Here he turned and walked to the left.)

What the speaker said is true. We are more than our bodies. God has made us so. Our bodies are worth a great deal, but they are to be cared for and used to serve good purposes. If we do this, we will be good stewards of our bodies. This is the Christian way of life.

There are many ways in which we can care for our bodies. God has made us in such a way that we require a certain amount of sleep. If we give our bodies, on the average, eight hours of sleep a night, our bodies will respond to our needs with marvelous strength.

The same is true of exercise. If we exercise our muscles regularly and sufficiently, we are able to do much more, more comfortably, than when we allow our muscles to become flabby. Adequate breathing exercises keep the blood aerated, thus giving us the vigor we need to enjoy life.

We can care for our bodies by what we do, or do not, put into them. God made us in such a way that we need a balanced diet if we are to function as we should. Three times a day at mealtime (and often between meals) we have a chance to show that we care for ourselves by what we eat or don't eat. Our bodies also need a certain amount of liquid each day if all the parts are to function well. Growing boys and girls need a great deal of water and milk. Making sure that our bodies get the liquid they need will show whether or not we care for ourselves. But the kind of liquid taken in also shows this, for some kinds are upbuilding while others are destructive. Alcoholic beverages have been causing trouble for quite a while, as the following quotation, written more than two thousand years ago, shows:

> Wine is a mocker, strong drink a brawler,
> and whoever is led astray by it is not wise.
> —Proverbs 20:1

Being good stewards of our bodies requires us to think about such things and to regulate what goes into our bodies.

When we are sick, our doctor prescribes drugs to make us well. Taking them into our bodies in well-regulated doses does much good, but taking in more than is needed can do much harm and even cause death. There are certain drugs, such as cocaine, that cause people to lose control of themselves. These drugs control the body to such an extent that people become wild unless they can satisfy their body's craving for more.

Tobacco is something else that makes some people lose control of their bodies. They light one cigarette after the other. They develop a craving that demands satisfaction in another smoke. Nicotine, a chemical in tobacco, is more addictive than alcohol and many other drugs. Those addicted are no longer in control of their bodies.

God has made sex a very important part of the stewardship of our bodies. Through sex the human race is perpetuated. Much satisfaction and joy in life can result from it. It can be very sacred, but it can also be so degraded that it becomes sordid. Christian stewardship requires that we use our sex impulses to express care and love, not power or control.

Your class might like to draw up a set of guidelines for the Christian care of the body—guidelines that express your stewardship of one of the most precious things God has given you.

Care for Your Money

Money is a good thing, but it may also be harmful. Read in 1 Timothy 6:10 what Paul says about the love of money. We can use money for our own good, for our neighbor's good, and for doing God's work in the world. But if we let money be our god, then we need to be reminded of something Jesus said: "You cannot serve God and wealth."

Money itself is neither good nor bad. It is how we use it that is good or bad. Money is something over which Christians must exercise good stewardship. Money represents life and work. It can be exchanged for many things. What people exchange it for is important. If people exchange it for things that are worthwhile or for services that are helpful to others, they keep control of it; but if they spend it on harmful things, if they use it to indulge themselves in satisfying their every whim, if they waste it on frivolities or in gambling, or even if they hoard it, they will soon find that money controls them.

In a junior high church school class the teacher asked the members how much money they had to use, where they got it, and what they did with it. Which of the answers given in the following paragraphs do you think comes closest to the Christian way of using one's money? Why do you think so? Did any of these young people seem to have a feeling of Christian responsibility for spending money wisely? Did any feel responsibility to God for using some of their money to help others?

Carlton didn't receive an allowance, but he had a part-time job after school. He used his money to buy clothes and Nintendo games. His grades had fallen, so he thought the reason might be that he worked too many hours; he did not have much time to study and complete his homework assignments.

Courtney had an allowance of ten dollars a week. She spent it any way she chose—usually at her favorite fast-food restaurant or on tapes of her favorite recording star. Every Saturday her father gave her the allowance. Courtney said she thought her parents made too much fuss over how she spent her allowance.

Kyle lived in a rural area. He said he did not receive an allowance, but he had a paper route. He saved most of his money because he wanted to attend college. He said his parents made him use some of his earnings for church offerings. He didn't particularly want to do this, but he did it anyway.

Rachel received five dollars a week in allowance. About once a week, she earned ten dollars babysitting. She was brought up learning how to tithe, so she always put 10 percent of her allowance and earnings in her church offering. Rachel also saved a portion of her money. The rest of her money was spent on clothes and other things she wanted that she didn't want to ask her parents for.

Chris was the money saver. He had an allowance of twenty dollars a week, most of which he saved. Chris's parents also gave him two dollars for every A and one dollar for every B he received on his report card. He put this money in his savings account. During the summer he mowed his neighbors' lawns and saved this money too. Chris had no particular plans for his money, but he liked knowing that he had a lot of money in the bank if he ever needed it.

Care for Your Time

Time is what life is made of. We have only so much. When it is gone, nothing can bring it back. Therefore we must learn to care for ourselves in the use of it. There are many questions that young people should face regarding the Christian use of time. Here are a few:

1. Most of your time is taken up with sleeping, dressing, eating, and attending school. Suppose that there are forty-four hours left each week—twelve on Saturday, twelve on Sunday, and four each weekday evening. How could these forty-four hours be divided among the following:

( ) helping in the home

( ) self-improvement—
music lessons, etc.

( ) working at a part-time job
( ) school studies
( ) hobbies

( ) having a good time
( ) spending time at the mall
( ) church services and activities

2. Some ways of having a good time are better than others. How many hours a week do you spend on each of the following? How many hours time might you spend?

Attending movies ( ) ( )   Visiting with friends ( ) ( )
Listening to the radio ( ) ( )   Walking or hiking ( ) ( )
Watching TV ( ) ( )   Going to Parties ( ) ( )
Taking part in sports ( ) ( )   Hobbies ( ) ( )
Watching sports ( ) ( )   Playing video games ( ) ( )
Reading books,   Surfing the internet ( ) ( )
    magazines, and   Talking on your
    papers ( ) ( )   cell phone ( ) ( )
Using your iPod ( ) ( )

3. With some of these activities, the important question is not how much time we spend on them, but what they are like. Consider movies, for example. There are all kinds of movies—horror movies, crime movies, mystery movies, romance movies, great books turned into movies, musical comedy movies. What movies have you seen that have helped you on your Christian journey? Which ones have hindered you?

A vast variety of entertainment is available today. Cable TV has opened the doors to all-news, all-sports, and all-movie channels as well as all-music channels. You can enjoy compact discs, walkman radios, and numerous types of television programs, such as soap operas and situation comedies. What are your favorite programs? Weigh them from a Christian point of view.

The same is true for reading. There are all sorts of reading materials—comics, teen magazines, romance novels, health and fitness magazines, adult magazines, religious books, and literary classics. What do you read? What types of reading materials have helped you as a Christian?

4. What rules could a Christian follow in regard to the way he or she spends his or her time?

Care for Your Life

Some of you may think that you cannot take care of yourselves now. Your parents and teachers tell you what to do. Yet you very definitely can care for your life. You can decide how you will live within the restrictions placed on you.

You can decide the kind of person you will be. You yourself will decide whether you will obey your parents, whether you will let your relations with boyfriends or girlfriends get out of control, or whether you will cheat on your schoolwork. You yourself will decide whether or not you will be friendly at school. You yourself will decide whether or not you will be kind to all people with whom you come in contact. You yourself will decide whether or not to accept Christ as your Savior and to follow his way of life. Being a good steward of your life right now is very important.

But it is also important for you to think of your future. What kind of person do you want to be? What kind of parent or partner will you be? What kind of work will you do? What would you like to do?

Many boys and girls of confirmation age already know what vocation they want to pursue, and they are working toward it. Ted loves music. It is his very life, so he spends every available minute practicing. He is looking forward to the time when he can go to one of the summer music camps. He is finding out about the various schools and colleges that specialize in music. He hopes to become a member of a great orchestra some day. Kathy has always enjoyed writing. Her stories always impress her friends. She has already submitted articles to her local newspaper. Kathy plans to take a writing course in high school and would like to major in journalism in college.

But there are many boys and girls of confirmation age who do not know as yet what their lifework will be. They are dreaming about various fields. Some might one day aspire to become administrative assistants, insurance salespeople, astronauts, computer technicians, police officers, fire fighters, taxi drivers, detectives, reporters, lawyers, ministers, teachers, professional athletes, or entertainers. They may be reading up on all the vocations they can to see if one is interesting to them.

There are still other boys and girls who just drift along, giving no thought beyond the day with its pleasures. Someday they will take any job that opens up to them, whether it is the work that can make them happy or not, and they may drift from one job to another.

How can you care for your life? What rules can you lay down for choosing your lifework in a Christian way? Does the matter of stewardship enter in here too?

Christians Get Back More Than They Give Up

Some people have the idea that to be Christian means principally to give up pleasures that non-Christians can enjoy. They say, "Christians can't do this" and "Christians can't do that." They assume that the life of a Christian is devoid of anything enjoyable.

As a matter of fact, there are some things that Christians cannot do or will not do. There are some things that Christians give up. But why? To achieve more true happiness than they could if they continued in their old ways. If Christians give up going to see movies that are contrary to the teachings of Christ, it is because they are sure that they cannot be the finest type of Christian they ought to be if they let movies lead their thoughts into evil. They know that would be contrary to God's will, and so they find good times that will leave a good taste in their mouth and that will truly re-create them in body, mind, and spirit.

Christians do not discipline themselves just to prove that they can. They do it for a purpose. They want to get the most out of life and to see that others have a chance to do the same. They wants to be fit for God's work. They are in training—not to run a race or play a game, but to live a full and useful life.

A Good Resolution

The following words were written by a young man named Howard Arnold Walter who went to Japan to do Christian work among students. A letter from his mother set him thinking, and he wrote a poem of resolution that has been of great help to many young people. Can you make it your own resolution?

> *I would be true, for there are those who trust me;*
> *I would be pure, for there are those who care;*
> *I would be strong, for there is much to suffer;*
> *I would be brave, for there is much to dare.*
>
> *I would be friend of all—the foe, the friendless;*
> *I would be giving, and forget the gift;*
> *I would be humble, for I know my weakness;*
> *I would look up, and laugh, and love, and lift.*

13

Christians Seek the Realm of God

Many, many times in the New Testament we find the words the kingdom of *God, the kingdom of heaven,* or simply the *kingdom.* They all mean the same thing. All look forward to a day when God's reign is accepted by all people, and God's will is done "on earth as it is in heaven." Perhaps reign or realm is better than kingdom, which is likely to make us think too much of so many square miles of land. The main idea of the kingdom is that God will reign.

This phrase, *the kingdom of God,* is nowhere to be found in the Old Testament, but its central idea is there. People even then hoped for the day when God's rule would go into effect more widely. Such a hope is seen in Micah 4:1–4. Turn to this passage in your Bible and see what Micah wrote about the reign of the Lord.

The coming of God's rule is still our hope—the greatest hope of Christians. God's realm has been coming through the years, but slowly. We look for its continued coming—more and more people accepting God's rule in their lives; more and more people yielding their lives to God; more and more kindness and sympathy and unselfishness in the world; less and less hatred and poverty and cruelty.

It is God's realm, but it comes through us and we can help its coming. We will never see it fully, but we will see more of it than we do now. Christians work and pray for it. The church works and prays for it the noblest dream that ever entered into the minds of humans. But first it was in the mind of God.

Jesus Sought to Bring Forth the Realm of God

All of Jesus' life centers on the realm of God. One does not realize this until one takes, for example, the Gospel of Matthew and pages through it to see how often Jesus speaks of God's realm. Underline lightly in your Bible every time Matthew reports that Jesus spoke of God's realm. Then look up the following passages and answer the questions listed. All this will help you to understand what the realm of God meant to Jesus.

Matthew 4:17. What was Jesus' message when he began to preach?

Matthew 6:10. For what did he teach his disciples to pray?

Matthew 10:7. What was the central theme that Jesus gave his disciples for their preaching? _____

Matthew 18:4. Who is the greatest in God's realm? _____

Luke 17:20–21. Where is God's realm? _____

Many of Jesus' parables were told to help people understand what he meant by God's realm. He compared it to many things. Read the following comparisons and write what you think Jesus meant by them.

Matthew 13:3–8

Matthew 13:33

Matthew 25:1–13

From your research in the Bible you can get some idea of the importance to Jesus of God's realm. He himself was living in it, and he wanted everyone else to have the joy of living in it also. Therefore the bringing forth of the realm was on his mind and in his heart constantly. He preached about it. He taught about it. He worked for it. He lived for it. He died for it.

We Should Seek God's Realm

Jesus has made it clear that we too should seek God's realm—so clear that we cannot possibly misunderstand. In Matthew 6:33 we have his command to seek first the realm of God. What does this mean?

1.	*It means that we are to think more about God's realm than about anything else.* How much time do you now spend thinking about sports? clothes? movies? the realm of God? Is it too much to expect of young people that they should spend more time thinking about the day when God's rule will be acknowledged over all the earth than about their own needs and pleasures? Do you think that Jesus meant for young people to obey this command, or was it only for older people?

2.	*It means that we are to work harder for the realm of God than for anything else.* How much time do you now spend working for God's realm? A good many things can come under this head. All church work can be counted, if one is trying to do God's will in it. All schoolwork can be counted, if one is trying to do God's will in it. Athletics can probably be counted, if one is trying to do God's will in them. Is it too much to expect of young people that they should work harder for God's realm than for their own pleasure? Or is God's realm for older people only?

3.	*It means that we are to put God's realm at the top of the list of things we want in life.* What do you want? A good time? Popularity? Success? Money? What do you want more than anything else in the world? Is it too much to expect of young people that they should put God's realm at the top of the list of their interests and desires? Do you think that our Lord meant for young people to do this, or only for those over forty?

4.	*It means that we are to bear God's realm in mind as we meet the ordinary challenges of life.* An examination comes along in school, and the temptation to cheat is strong. What way of acting will be most in keeping with God's will? What way of acting will bring nearer the day when God's rule will be acknowledged by all?

Probably, there are in your community people and families of another race or nationality than your own. The young members of such families may come to your school or your church, or you may pass them on the street. How should you act toward them if you are trying to do God's will? How should you act to bring nearer the day when God's rule will be acknowledged by all?

Is it asking too much of young people that they should bear God's realm in mind as they meet the ordinary challenges of life?

5. *Seeking God's realm means that we are to bear it in mind as we choose a vocation.* Which of the following occupations could a person select with the feeling that she or he was doing God's will and was bringing nearer the day when God's rule would be acknowledged everywhere?

Salesclerk	Teacher	Drug dealer
Physician	Military officer	Baker
Homemaker	Coal miner	Police officer
Farmer	Fashion designer	Editor
Insurance salesperson	Musician	Politician
Auto mechanic	Bartender	Writer
News anchor	Worker in a steel mill	Actor
Minister	Pilot	Union officer

Are any of these in keeping with God's will only if done in a certain way? Are any of them always in keeping with the will of God? Are any of them never in keeping with it? Give reasons for your answers.

6. *It means that we are to have God's realm in mind when we join the church.* The church is where God's will is already being done in part, and where people work for the day when it will be done everywhere more perfectly. To become a full member of the church means to seek God's realm more than one has ever sought it before.

Is God's will being done more fully in the churches of your community than in the schools, the places of business, the video arcades? Give reasons for your answer.

Do the churches of your community do more than other institutions and business to bring forth the day when God's rule will be acknowledged everywhere? Give reasons for your answer.

7. *Seeking first the realm of God means that we are to find our greatest joy in losing ourselves in some good work.* The good work may be something truly big, like seeking world peace, working for a better understanding between people of different races and various ethnic groups, or doing away with poverty and homelessness. It may be teaching young children, making a happy home, or caring for the sick people of a community. At any rate, we never

know what true happiness is until we have forgotten ourselves completely in some good work. The truth of this is clearly seen in the four people whose lives we looked at briefly in chapter 11: Martin Luther King, Jr., Albert Schweitzer, Florence Nightingale, and Mother Teresa. Think about their lives.

Their way is not the easiest way to live or the easiest way to find happiness, but it is the Christian way.

The Cost of the Christian Way of Life

There is no use shutting our eyes to the fact that the Christian way of life costs something to those who follow it. Christians must give up some things that others can do. They must do some things and believe some things that others will not like. They may not make as much money as some others. They may not be as popular as some others.

Time and again Jesus warned his disciples that the Christian way is not an easy way. Here is what he said: "If any want to become my followers, let them deny themselves and take up their cross and follow me" (Matthew 16:24). This is a strange way to win followers, but Jesus believed in facing all the facts. The Christian way led him to an actual cross. Sooner or later all true followers of his will find some kind of cross in their path. But it is worth it! Hebrews 12:2 says that Jesus "for the sake of the joy that was set before him endured the cross." The prophets, the martyrs, and the saints of all ages have found that the Christian way of life is always worth more than it costs.

On Being a Christian

Write here a description of a person who is practicing the Christian way of life. Make this positive by saying what he or she is or does rather than what he or she is not or does not do. Feel free to express yourself in poetry rather than prose, if you like.

PART FOUR
The Christian Church

14
The Story of the Christian Church

The church is more than a building or any number of buildings. It is more than your home congregation. It is more than our United Church of Christ. We are only one denomination, and there are many others. It is more than all the Christians in the United States. The word church comes from a Greek word meaning "belonging to the Lord." The church is all those in every land and in every age who are the Lord's.

How many Christians are there in the world now? No one knows exactly, but perhaps one-third of all the people on the earth consider themselves Christians. Can you picture them? They are young and old, rich and poor, white, black, red, yellow, and brown, ignorant and educated. All these characteristics, however, do not matter. The nations in which these people live may even go to war with one another, but they still belong to one church. The church, then, reaches all around the earth. It reaches back into the past to Jesus himself, and it will reach, we believe, far into the future.

The Long Story of the Church

There was a time when there was no United Church of Christ, no Roman Catholic church, no church of any kind. There were no church buildings, no Christian ministers, no Christian Bible, no Christian hymns, no Christians. How did it call come to be? For the sake of convenience we will divide the story of the church into four periods of about five hundred years each. The tree of the Christian church on the next page will help you to picture the church's growth.

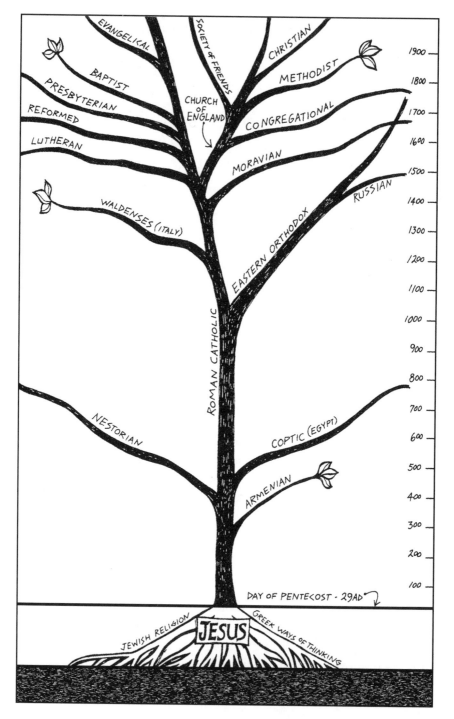

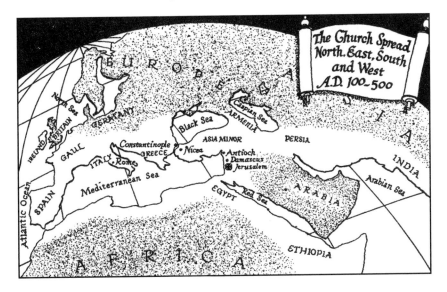

The Church Spread
North, East, South
and West
A.D. 100-500

Period I

(The church took shape and spread through the Roman Empire.)

The church began, of course, with Jesus. He gathered about him a few disciples. They found God through him. Their whole lives were changed by him. For a little while he was with them in the body. Then he was crucified and died. On the third day he arose, and for a while his disciples were aware of his presence in various times and places. Then he was gone.

On the fiftieth day after his resurrection came the Jewish holiday of Pentecost. This was the birthday of the Christian church. On this great day the disciples were together in Jerusalem, talking no doubt about Jesus. Then something happened to them and in them. They were convinced beyond all doubt that the God whom they had seen so clearly in Jesus was still present with them. They called this presence the Holy Spirit. They were almost beside themselves with joy. You can see this for yourself as you read the second chapter of Acts. On this day many were added to the community of the disciples of Jesus Christ. This community held everything in common. They had the same beliefs about Jesus and God. They met together for worship in the temple, as other Jews did, but they also met in one another's homes to pray and to break bread as Jesus had done at the Last Supper. They even put all their money into a common treasury.

Soon the Christians began to scatter because of the persecutions in Jerusalem. They went north, east, south, and west. Some went north to Antioch, which became the second center from which Christian teaching went out. Some went east to Persia and beyond. (The Mar Thoma Church in India claims as its founder the apostle Thomas.) Others went west across Asia Minor into Greece and on into Italy, France, and Spain; still others went across northern Africa into Egypt and Ethiopia until the church had spread all around the Mediterranean Sea and even as far as Ireland.

By A.D. 200 there was a church organization running from southern France to the Tigris and Euphrates valleys in Asia. Across northern Africa half the people were Christians. About the year 250 a letter was written about the church at Rome. It said that there was a bishop at Rome, with forty-six presbyters and seven deacons under him. In addition, there were more than one hundred other officers and thirty thousand church members. The church was strong enough and rich enough and good enough to care for fifteen hundred poor people. What a marvelous growth from the little beginnings by the Sea of Galilee!

How did this take place? We believe that God had much to do with it, and that God worked through missionaries, one of whom was Paul. A large part of the book of Acts tells of Paul's life and work. He is one of the greatest people in the history of the church.

Before becoming a Christian, Paul had persecuted Christians with all the strength he had. But the way they lived and died made a great impression on him, so great that when Christ called him to become his follower he was ready to give his life to his new Lord. (See Acts 26:12–18.) For about twenty years Paul told the good news of God's love in Jesus Christ across Asia Minor, in Macedonia and Greece, and finally in Rome. You can read his own account of the hardships of those years in 2 Corinthians 11:23–28.

But the church spread in other ways as well. Ordinary people—slaves, soldiers, merchants—became Christians and told the good news. Strange as it may seem, the church also spread through persecution. If a group of Christians had to flee for their lives, they carried the good news wherever they went. One chief reason for the spread of the church was the way the Christians lived. Not many were rich and powerful people. Most lived fine lives and died noble deaths, and this was a powerful argument. Then, too, the Roman world was hungry for good news about life, and Christianity spoke to the longings of many a heart.

All this sounds as though these early centuries were easy ones for the Christians. They were not. Time and again the Christians were persecuted. Stephen was the first Christian martyr (read Acts 6:8–8:1). Romans ruled the Mediterranean and much of Europe, and they did not know what to do with these Christians who would not worship the Roman emperor, serve as soldiers, or attend the shows where men had to fight each other to the death, and they treated slaves with a strange kindness. So the Romans persecuted them. They took the wealth of the Christians. They took their church properties. They forbade them to meet together. They sent them into exile. They killed them by the thousands. During the first two hundred years there were persecutions here and there, but in the third and the beginning of the fourth centuries there were persecutions that ran from one end of the empire to the other.

All this came to an end with the Emperor Constantine. The story goes that in a battle just above Rome on October 28, 312, he saw a cross in the skies with the words (in Latin) "In this sign conquer." The next year, 313, he signed an order that put Christianity on a level with any other religion of the empire. Christians no longer had to be afraid. They could say anywhere that they were followers of Christ. Their Lord's Day (Sunday) was made a holiday by law. The Christian cross was stamped on Roman coins. From then on it was much easier to be a Christian, sometimes too easy.

During these early centuries there were many things to be decided and settled. We have already seen how the books of the New Testament were chosen and how the Apostles' Creed and Nicene Creed came to be (see pages 14, 61, 64).

A form of worship had to be worked out also. In the earliest days Christians simply came together each Sunday in one another's houses. They read from the Old Testament and later from Paul's letters and the Gospels. They heard a sermon. They prayed. Then they ate a meal together, which included a service of communion as their Lord had instituted it on that last night in Jerusalem. Little by little the Lord's Supper was separated from the meal and became the main part of their worship.

The early church also had to find officers, or leaders. In the first church at Jerusalem the leaders were the twelve apostles, who had been closest to the Lord and would be best able to guide the church.

In Acts 6:1–6 you will find the beginnings of a new office, that of deacon. (A deacon serves by helping church members.) In Acts 11:30 elders are mentioned. (An elder is an older leader who assists the pastor in the running of the church.) In time the leading elder in a region began to oversee the work of the whole area. This person became known as bishop. (A bishop is an overseer of a number of churches.) The bishop of a strong church in a large city had more influence than other bishops. The bishop of Rome came to have the most influence because people had long been used to thinking of Rome as the center of the world. So the bishop of Rome became in time the head of the whole church. He was called pope, which means "father" (similar to our word papa).

The early Christians also had to decide exactly what they believed. They knew well enough that in Jesus they had found God and all that made life worthwhile, but to put that into words was another matter. And so they thought hard and argued a good deal. Constantine, however, wanted good feeling throughout his empire. So he called three hundred bishops together at Nicea (near Constantinople) in the year 325 in the first great council. The Nicene Creed reflects what this council agreed on.

It was during these early centuries that the practice of slipping away from the evil of the world and living alone began. The people who did this were called monks. The first real monk, named Anthony, was born in Egypt about 250. He read what Jesus said to the bright young ruler in Matthew 19:21: "If you would be perfect, go, sell what you possess and give to the poor." So Anthony went out into the Egyptian desert to live alone, fasting and spending much time in prayer. Many other sincere Christians did likewise in the years that followed.

There were many great names during these years. There was Ulfilas, who in the fourth century went as a missionary to the Germanic tribes along the Danube River, in what is now Bulgaria. There was Patrick, who was a missionary to Ireland in the fifth century (and whom we think of in connection with Saint Patrick's Day). There were wise teachers, great preachers, and able bishops. Perhaps the greatest of them all in this period was Augustine. He was born in northern Africa in the year 354. As a youth he was brilliant, but not at all serious. One day while he was sitting in a garden he heard a child saying, over and over, "Take up and read." He saw a New Testament on a bench, picked it up and his glance fell on two verses in Romans that seemed to fit him exactly. (Read Romans 13:13–14 and see if you can tell why these verses had a message for Augustine.) They set him to thinking about his life, and he decided to become a Christian. One of his books is *The City of God*. By this he meant the company of God's faithful people in the church. It was this "City of God" that Augustine was sure would grow in strength. He was right. In 476, not many years after Augustine's death, the city of Rome fell, but the City of God was strong and becoming stronger.

The Story of the Christian Church

Period II
(The church spread farther and kept witnessing in the face of opposition.)

A king and queen had much to do with the conversion of the Franks, from whom France gets its name. Queen Clotilde (who became Saint Clotilde) was a Christian, but her husband, King Clovis, was not until Christmas day, 496, when he was baptized at Rheims. In those days, when rulers were baptized, many of their followers also were, whether they really wanted to be Christians or not.

Augustine (not the same man who came from northern Africa) was sent as a missionary to England by Pope Gregory. Why to England? The story goes that in the slave market Gregory had seen some youths. He asked who they were. The reply was "Angles" (Englishmen). "Not Angles, but angels," Gregory is supposed to have said. The story may or may not be true, but it is certainly true that he sent Augustine to England in 596.

Boniface, an Englishman of the eighth century, was a missionary to the Germans. In the region that we now know as Holland he was killed by unfriendly people.

Ansgar, in the ninth century, became a missionary to the Norse peoples. He preached in Denmark and Sweden.

Christianity came to Russia in the tenth century, from the eastern part of the church in Constantinople. The real beginning was when the Grand Duke Vladimir I was baptized in 988. Many years later the Russian church became autocephalous (self-governing), as the "tree" on page 98 shows.

But this is not the end of the story. As far back as the seventh century one branch of the church carried the good news of Jesus to south India and even to China. About the time the Mayflower sailed to America, workers in China discovered a stone that was then at least 800 years old. The carving on it speaks of the Trinity, the birth of Jesus, the visit of the Wise Men, and the sacrament of baptism, and it even mentions that there are twenty-seven books in the New Testament. How the church spread is truly wonderful—is it not?

In Europe these were difficult days. The Roman Empire was gone, and the European peoples were only slowly giving up some of their crude ways. The church's buildings and monasteries were signs of hope in a time of despair, like stars in the night sky. Imperfect as it was, the church shed much light. The worship of God was carried on. Children were taught. Books were copied. The sick were cared for. Some efforts were made to stop the constant warring. The light that came into the world with Jesus was kept burning.

Period III
(The church reached the peak of its power and began to decline.)

The eastern half of the church and the western half had been drifting apart for some time. They could not agree on the use of images in the churches, nor on many other matters. In 1054 the pope in Rome declared that the eastern half of the church was no longer a part of the true church. Of course, the church in the east did not agree, but from that time on the church was divided into the Roman Catholic church and the Eastern Orthodox church. (There had been a few smaller splits, as the illustration on page 98 points out, but the great majority of Christians had belonged to the one great church up to this time.)

The western church grew in power, and the pope came to rival the emperor. When Gregory VII was pope and Henry IV emperor, there arose a dispute over who had the right to appoint bishops. The pope ruled that the emperor was no longer in the church, and all his subjects could rebel against him. So powerful was the pope in 1077 that the emperor came to northern Italy to the town of Canossa, where the pope was staying, and stood before the gate three days in his bare feet during the cold of winter to make peace. The church had come a long way from the lowly Jesus. This marked almost the peak of the church's power—but not quite. Innocent III, one hundred years later, was probably the most powerful of all the popes. He actually made the king of England pay taxes to him, as though England belonged to the pope.

One of the best known activities of the church during these years was the Crusades. The Turks had taken the Holy Land and Christians were kept from going to see the places where Jesus had walked the earth. Gregory VII received a call from the eastern emperor to help him against the Turks. All through Europe people gathered together for the task of setting the Holy Land free. In the two hundred years from 1096 to 1272 there were a number of Crusades. By land and by sea the Crusaders made their way to the Holy Land. They captured Jerusalem but did not hold it. Many thousands of people were killed in the battles. In fact, the Crusades did little good except to bring the people of Europe in touch with new places and new ideas. One sad part of the story of the Crusades is that of the Children's Crusade. A boy in France and another in Germany called children together for a crusade of their own. Slave traders got the French children into ships by offering to take them to Palestine, but they instead sold them as slaves in Egypt. Most of the children from Germany perished as they crossed the Alps into Italy, and the remainder were turned back by the pope.

On the "tree" on page 98 there is a branch called the Waldenses. They were a group of Christians named for Peter Waldo, a rich merchant in southern France. Like Anthony years before, he read Jesus' words to the rich young man and followed them. This was in 1176. He and his followers aroused the displeasure of the Roman Catholic church and then suffered severe persecution for their beliefs and deeds. The people who examined them were called Inquisitors. The organization that did this work was called the Inquisition. In the years that followed, many others besides the Waldenses suffered at the hands of the Inquisition.

One of the truest Christians of this age or any other was Giovanni Bernadone, better known as Francis of Assisi. He was born in 1181 or 1182, the son of a well-to-do merchant. Like Augustine, he was a carefree young man, and like Augustine he changed into a great Christian. One day he took some cloth from one of his father's storehouses and sold it to rebuild a church near his home. This was the beginning of a life that led to little money but many acts of kindness. Saint Francis thought of himself as a brother to every living thing, even birds and animals. The hymn "All Creatures of Our God and King" was written by him and shows his spirit. His followers were called Franciscans. They pledged themselves to a life of poverty and service to others.

At about the same time another famous order of monks was started by a Spaniard named Dominic. Hence they were called Dominicans. Many of them became great preachers and professors in universities. Other monastic communities followed, some for women as well as men.

The great pope Innocent III was in power when the thirteenth century started. The Crusades were in full swing. Francis and Dominic were carrying out their work. Thomas Aquinas, the great thinker of the Roman Catholic church, lived in this century. Universities began to spring up in Europe about this time. Great cathedrals had already been started, with whole communities joining in the work of building these beautiful houses of God.

It is difficult to remain humble before God and kind to others when things are going well. The church was strong, rich, and powerful, but it had also become rigid and oppressive. In the fourteenth century people began to think of righting some of the wrongs in the church.

John Wyclif tried to do this in England. He believed that the Bible should be the one guide that the church should try to follow. Because the people could not read the Latin Bible in use in the churches, he translated the Bible into English. He also said that the church was not made of its high officials only, but of all of Christ's followers.

At about the same time there lived in Bohemia another John. John Hus read what John Wyclif wrote and held many of the same views. He also opposed the sale of indulgences. The Roman Catholic church held that the goodness of Christ and the saints was stored up as in a bank, and some of it could be checked out to save sinners from punishment they would otherwise receive. People could get this stored-up goodness by paying money to the church—by buying indulgences. Hus thought this was wrong. His views did not please the Roman Catholic church, and he was burned at the stake.

New ideas were stirring. The Renaissance, or "rebirth" of interest in life here and now rather than in salvation for a future life, was starting. Before long, Columbus would sail to the New World. The Middle Ages were over.

Period IV
(The church divided into many branches and spread around the world.)

Did it not seem strange to you when you looked at the "tree" on page 98 that so many churches branched off from the Roman Catholic church at about the same time? These branches are all Protestant churches. (They protested against the practices of the Roman Catholic church.) The followers of Martin Luther were the first to break away and form a new church. Luther had been a monk in the Catholic church but could not seem to find peace of mind no matter how much he tried. He had studied the writings of Augustine and also the Bible. Gradually he had come to understand that people are not saved by their good deeds but by God's gracious love. He believed that Christians should put their faith in this great love of God. When John Tetzel came to Germany to sell indulgences and said that as soon as the money hit the collection box some soul would be saved, Luther nailed on the church door at Wittenberg a paper on which were ninety-five statements that he was willing to debate. This act started the Protestant Reformation (a period of reforming, or making over, the church).

Meanwhile to the south in Switzerland, a man named Ulrich Zwingli was saying about the same thing. He too was a priest. He too went back to the Bible as the only rule of faith and life for Christians. He too believed that people were saved "by grace through faith." By 1522 he was preaching his ideas in the town of Zurich so that all could hear. In 1523 he prepared sixty-seven statements of his own. As Luther was the founder of all Lutheran churches, Zwingli was the founder of all Reformed and Presbyterian churches. Several new branches of the church were begun.

These two men are of special interest to us because the Evangelical and Reformed part of our United Church of Christ can be traced back to them. They met once at Marburg in 1529. They could agree on most things, but not quite on the Lord's Supper. So the two branches went their separate ways. The Lutheran church grew in Germany, Denmark, Norway, Sweden, and America. The Reformed church grew in southern Germany, France, Holland, Scotland, and America.

In some places this latter branch was called Presbyterian (governed by presbyters, or elders). All Reformed and Presbyterian people owe much to two other men besides Zwingli. Both were named John. John Calvin worked out the Reformed and Presbyterian beliefs better than any other person has ever done. John Knox was a fiery Scotchman who served nineteen months as a galley slave because of his Protestant beliefs. In Geneva he became a follower of Calvin, and later he did much to make Scotland Protestant.

Now a word about the other branches. The Baptists came from some friends of Zwingli in Zurich who felt that he did not go far enough. They did not believe in baptizing children. They felt it was better to wait until people were old enough to make promises for themselves. The Baptist teachings spread in Germany and Holland, but mostly in England and America.

For many years the English people had resisted being ruled by the pope in matters of religion. About this time Henry VIII, ruler of England, wanted to divorce his wife and marry another. The pope would not agree to the divorce, so in 1533 Henry broke with him. The next year Parliament set the English church entirely free of the pope and placed it under the English monarch. Out of the Church of England came our American Episcopal churches. (*Episcopal* means "ruled by bishops.")

Meanwhile in England there were those who wanted more than just to be free from the pope. They wanted to make the church "pure" of many Roman Catholic practices. These people were the Puritans. For example, they did not like the fine robes of the priests because these robes seemed to set the priests apart from ordinary members. From the Puritans came the Congregational branch of our United Church of Christ. The first Congregational church was started by Robert Browne in 1581. The Pilgrims on the *Mayflower* were Congregationalists.

The chief founder of the Methodist branch was John Wesley. He was the son of a minister of the Church of England. While studying at Oxford, he, with his brother Charles and others, formed a club. They were nicknamed *Methodists* because they planned their daily lives with such detailed method. On the evening of May 24, 1738, John Wesley was sitting in a meeting in London. Some of Luther's writings were being read. Suddenly he felt sure that he was saved by Christ. The next year he organized the first Methodist congregation. The Methodist church, like its founder, has made much of what a Christian feels in her or his heart. This church reached the middle-class people of England with the Christian gospel, and it has become strong in America.

Many other branches of the church were started in Europe, such as the Quakers and the Moravians, and some of their members came to America. Here new branches were added, such as the Disciples of Christ. Now there are more than two hundred Protestant denominations in America.

When all these branches began to appear in the sixteenth century, the Roman Catholic church increased its own efforts to remain a force in Christian affairs. It purified itself from within. It persecuted the Protestants. It sent missionaries into other countries. Thus this church remains strong to-day in many lands.

About the year 1800 the Protestant churches began their own missionary work. Many missionary societies were started. Money was raised, and brave men and women left their homes for the dangerous work of carrying the Christian faith to the uttermost parts of the earth.

The History of the Christian Church

Underline the answer that completes the sentence correctly.

1. The birthday of the Christian church is
   (a) Christmas.   (b) Easter.   (c) Pentecost.

2. The first Christians worshiped in
   (a) one another's homes.   (b) churches.
   (c) fields.   (d) the Temple.

3. Whenever they met together, the first Christians
   (a) sacrificed an animal.   (b) ate together.

4. The first great missionary to Europe was
   (a) Peter.   (b) Thomas.
   (c) Paul.   (d) Philip.

5. The early Christians
   (a) placed all their money and possessions in a common treasury.
   (b) kept their possessions for themselves.
   (c) gave a tenth to the church.

6. The first officers in the Christian churches were elders and
   (a) preachers.   (b) deacons.   (c) popes.

7. The early Christians would not worship
   (a) the emperor.   (b) God.

8. The first emperor to become Christian was
   (a) Julius Caesar.   (b) Marcus Aurelius.   (c) Constantine.

9. The council of churches and bishops meeting in the year 325 formulated the
   (a) Nicene Creed   (b) Apostles' Creed.

10. The bishop of Rome came to be called
    (a) presbyter.   (b) pope.   (c) elder.

11. The church was taken to England by
    (a) Augustine.   (b) Patrick.   (c) Gregory the Great.

12. A great missionary to the Germans was
    (a) Ansgar.   (b) Boniface.

13. The man who pledged himself and his followers to poverty and service was
    (a) Francis of Assisi. (b) Innocent III.   (c) Ulfilas.

14. The man who was burned at the stake because he wanted to reform the evils of the Catholic church was
    (a) John Wyclif.   (b) John Hus.   (c) Martin Luther.

15. The chief founder of the Reformed and Presbyterian churches was
    (a) Zwingli.   (b) Calvin.   (c) Luther.

16, The founder of the first Congregational church was
    (a) Robert Browne. (b) John Wesley.   (c) Henry VIII.

17. The first Congregationalists came to this country in
    (a) Santa Maria.   (b) Mayflower.   (c) Nina.

18. A denomination that grew up in the United States is
    (a) Disciples of Christ.
    (b) the Quakers.
    (c) the Episcopal church.

15

What Protestants Believe

Protestants are Christians first. Whether a Christian belongs to a Protestant church, to the Roman Catholic church, to the Eastern Orthodox church, or to any other Christian church, there are certain beliefs that are common to all. We have discussed these in detail in Part 2 (see pages 29–68). Briefly, all Christians believe in the following:

> God the Supreme Being, Maker of heaven and earth;
> Jesus Christ, God's Son, our Lord;
> The Holy Spirit, the Comforter;
> The holy universal (one, holy, catholic, apostolic) church;
> The communion of saints;
> The forgiveness of sins;
> The life everlasting;
> The realm of God.

There are also certain basic beliefs that Protestants alone hold. Reread the paragraphs on Luther and Zwingli in chapter 14 (page 107). Underline what each one believed that was different from the prevailing beliefs of the Roman Catholic church.

Protestants Believe in the Bible

Protestants believe that the Bible contains the Word of God, God's foundation for our faith and life. They believe that the Bible needs no other interpreter than the Holy Spirit. Believing that Bible study is necessary for Christian living, Protestants are always concerned about having the Bible available in the language of the people, in words that they can understand. They also help those who cannot read to learn to do so.

Protestants Believe in the Gospel

The gospel is the good news. It is good news about God, about humanity, about sin, about life, and about death. The good news about God is that God is love. The good news about humanity is that we are children of God, made in the image of God, free and immortal. The good news about sin is that sin can be forgiven. If we confess our sins directly to God, we will be forgiven and cleansed from all unrighteousness. God's forgiveness is full and free to all who turn to God in sincere repentance. This forgiveness is not conditioned by good works, merit, prayers to saints, or the words of pastor or priest. It is God who saves. It is Christ who died for us. We cannot save ourselves. God alone can save people and offer the abundant life that Christ has promised to all who respond in faith.

Protestants Believe in the Church

The church was founded by Jesus Christ. Christ is the head of the church. The church is his body. That is, it is through the church that Christ carries out his purpose in the world. The church is not primarily an organization. Rather, it is a society of believers, a community that gathers in the name of Christ. The church is the people of God. Wherever the gospel is preached and the sacraments are truly administered, there is the church.

Protestants Believe in Freedom of Worship

Protestants believe that every Christian has direct access to God through Christ. They believe in the "priesthood of believers." They believe that each believer in God can approach God directly for personal petitions and to intercede on behalf of others. No particular place and no special form of worship is required. Nor must the approach to God be made through a minister or a priest. This does not mean that Protestants have no need of ministers, but that each Christian must be free to worship God as he or she desires.

What Our Denomination Believes

The United Church of Christ is a Protestant church, a branch of the one Christian church. Our denomination has its roots in the Reformation and has grown, through its several branches, in the freedom that the United States has granted to its churches.

In the preamble to the constitution of the United Church of Christ, we find the following:

> The United Church of Christ acknowledges as its sole Head, Jesus Christ, Son of God and Savior. It acknowledges as kindred in Christ all who share in this confession. It looks to the Word of God in the Scriptures, and to the presence and power of the Holy Spirit, to prosper its creative and redemptive work in the world. It claims as its own the faith of the historic Church expressed in the ancient creeds and reclaimed in the basic insights of the Protestant Reformers. It affirms the responsibility of the Church in each generation to make this faith its own in reality of worship, in honesty of thought and expression, and in purity of heart before God. In accordance with the teaching of our Lord and the practice prevailing among evangelical Christians, it recognizes two sacraments; Baptism and the Lord's Supper or Holy Communion.

The Second General Synod of the United Church of Christ held in Oberlin, Ohio, in 1959 approved a Statement of Faith. This statement is found on pages 60–61.

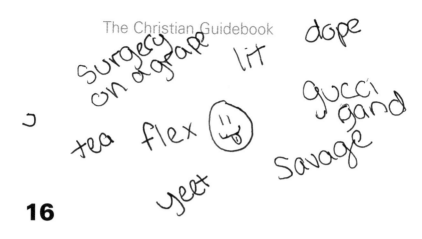

16

The Story of Our Denomination

Christians, by virtue of their baptism, all belong to the one Christian church. The branch in which we hold membership is the United Church of Christ. This is a union of two denominations, the Evangelical and Reformed church and the Congregational Christian churches. As the names indicate, each of these churches was formed by a union of other denominations.

The Congregational Part of Our Story

The story of Congregationalism begins in England at the end of the sixteenth century. The Church of England by that time had declared itself free of Rome, but there were many devout members of the Church of England who believed that it fell far short of the New Testament ideal. They felt certain that the cure for its sick condition was a return to the kind of church life described in the Bible. They found there a church in which all the believers had a share in its governance—wholly unlike the Church of England of that day, in which the authority was largely confined to the bishops, backed by the state. The people who felt unhappy about this situation began to preach the need for a church in which the members of all congregations had a voice.

Two Ideas For A New Testament-Type Church

There were two main ideas as to how such a church could come into being.

1. Many small groups called *Separatists* felt that the only way to reach this goal was to separate themselves from the Church of England, which they

regarded as having gone astray, and under their own government to carry on the true church of the real Christian tradition.

The beginnings of Congregationalism are usually dated from the founding of a church in Norwich in 1581 by the Separatist Robert Browne. He and his congregation were soon forced to leave England because of his bitter attacks on the Church of England. He and his followers emigrated to Holland.

In 1604 (the first year of the reign of James I) the Separatist pastor John Robinson came to a congregation already organized at Scrooby. It was chiefly because of him that Separatism did not narrow down into a little sect but broadened out into Congregationalism. He had been ordained in the Church of England, but he had become acquainted with Browne's writings and had accepted his principles but not his bitter attitude. For Robinson, too, exile became necessary. Together with a number of friends and followers he went first to Amsterdam and then to Leyden, Holland.

Although they met with a friendly reception there, they decided a few years later to move to America, where they could practice their Christianity unmolested and at the same time live and rear their children as English men and women. After many delays and discouragements, the first band of Separatists left Leyden. The Pilgrims, under the leadership of William Brewster, William Bradford, and Edward Winslow, landed at Plymouth, Massachusetts, in 1620. In this way the first Congregational church came to American soil.

2.   The second idea as to how to get back to a New Testament-type of church was held by the *Puritans*. They believed they could remain within the Church of England and from the inside purify that church. The majority believed that it would be enough of a reform if the churches were taken out of the hands of the bishops and put in the charge of committees of ministerial and lay leaders, or elders. These were Presbyterian Puritans. There was an active minority, however, who believed that the only thing to do was to go the whole distance and give an honest measure of church control to the people themselves—that is, a voice in the selection of their ministers, the management of their local churches, and the adoption of their own local creeds, or confessions. These were the Congregational Puritans, from among whom Massachusetts Bay was settled a few years after the Separatists had landed at Plymouth.

Beginnings In America

It was not long before the Puritans outnumbered the Pilgrims in New England by thousands. In England the two groups had been divided on the question as to whether they should work for reform from the inside or from outside of the Church of England; but in America, where there was no Church of England, this question did not arise, and they combined to form the Congregational churches.

The most important early meeting of the Congregational churches in New England was called the Cambridge Synod, after the Massachusetts town of the same name. Meeting in 1648, it drew up the Cambridge Platform, which was a description of church government and life that served the Congregational churches as a standard for two hundred years.

In those early years of New England, although the people had greater powers in the church than before, the pastors had the largest share of influence. When they had wrong ideas, the whole community was likely to follow them. So it was, for instance, in early Salem, when for a little time women charged with being witches were hanged. Fortunately, with the Bible as their guide, the pastors elsewhere were more often right than wrong, and the civilization they and their people established became a foundation for the United States of America. The basic principles on which our government was to be established 140 years later were set forth in 1636 by Thomas Hooker, the first minister of the Congregational church in Hartford, Connecticut.

Congregationalists Served In Many Ways

In the founding of our nation, Congregationalists had a notable part. Lay-persons like John Hancock and the Adamses were at the forefront of our national development in those critical early days. The democratic methods they had learned in their churches they now transferred to the state.

Congregationalists took their place not only in the world of action but also in the world of thought. Harvard College, the first college in America, was founded by Congregationalists in 1636. Jonathan Edwards, sometimes called the greatest systematic thinker America has produced, had a great effect on his generation. A religious revival known as the Great Awakening followed his preaching in Northampton, Massachusetts, beginning in 1734. His idea that thought is religion's best weapon, and religion is thought's best inspiration, was commonly accepted in Congregationalism. Congregationalists were great readers and writers of books.

A hundred years after Edwards, the Congregational minister Horace Bushnell of Hartford had an influence on American religion that is impossible to overestimate. Until his day, the churches tended to insist that a young person was not a Christian until after having a highly emotional "conversion," and they had built a system of revival meetings to induce such conversions. Against the excesses of this system Bushnell advanced the idea that "a child is to grow up a Christian and never know himself [or herself] otherwise."

Congregationalists did not keep the benefits of their thought and action to themselves. From the very beginning missionary work was emphasized. John Eliot, David Brainerd, and others influenced the American Indians. The missionary movement with which the Congregational churches as a whole were first identified was that which was fostered by the young Samuel J. Mills and his friends. The idea they conceived in 1806 at a prayer meeting held by a haystack in Williamstown, Massachusetts, led to the establishment of the American Board of Commissioners for Foreign Missions in 1810. This oldest of mission boards in the western hemisphere was united in 1961 with the Board of International Missions of the Evangelical and Reformed Church to form the United Church Board for World Ministries known today as Wider Church Ministries.

Congregationalists also pioneered in education, publishing, church extension, home missions, and social action.

The *Amistad* Event

On June 26, 1838, the ship *La Amistad* left the shores of Havana carrying 53 black Africans and their Spanish owners toward the United States. But three days out of port, the ordinary ship became the stage for an extraordinary event. Deciding to fight for their freedom, the Africans captured their ship and began to sail home—only to be recaptured and tried for murder and piracy.

Sengbe, who was known as Cinque by the Spanish, led the revolt in which the ship's captain was killed. Many New England Congregationalists understood that the teachings of Jesus Christ called for freedom for all people regardless of race or color. Their ancestors had once fled persecution themselves, and many continued to believe that individual liberty was God's great gift and intention for everyone.

A group known as the Amistad Committee was formed within a week of the ship's capture. The Committee wanted to free the Africans and ultimately to end slavery in the United States.

The committee's organizers included Lewis Tappan, a prosperous Evangelical abolitionist; Joshua Levitt, a lawyer and Congregational pastor who was the editor of *The Emancipator,* the journal of the American Anti-Slavery Society; and Simeon S. Jocelyn, also a Congregational minister.

The case moved from one court to the next and finally went to the Supreme Court. The Court decided in favor of the Africans. The Amistad Committee, which had shared the plight and the case of the captives with the American people throughout the proceedings, had raised funds to allow the Africans to realize their dream. The 35 survivors boarded a ship and returned to Africa.

Five years later, the Amistad Committee helped create the American Missionary Association, the first antislavery mission society on American soil. After the Civil War, the American Missionary Association founded schools and colleges throughout the South to educate newly freed slaves.

The Reformed Part of Our Story

The beginning of this story is on the continent of Europe. You remember that Ulrich Zwingli started the Reformed branch of the Christian church in Switzerland. Many German people, especially those who lived in the Rhine Valley just north of Switzerland, came to believe the Reformed teachings.

About 1700 these German people were finding life hard and bitter. The Thirty Years' War had caused great suffering. To make matters worse, Louis XIV of France sent his armies into the Rhineland and laid waste to it. Adding to the misery of the people was a succession of poor harvests for several years. Still worse, the winter of 1708–1709 was unusually severe. To top it all, a Roman Catholic became the ruler of the Palatinate, and Reformed people sometimes had to suffer for their faith. Their thoughts turned to America.

Beginnings In America

In the spring of 1709, a large number of German emigrants set out. Because of the favorable attitude of the government in Pennsylvania, many of the Reformed people settled in that area.

It was not easy for them to keep up their religious life in the new world, but they wanted to do it very much. Sometimes, when there was no minister in a struggling community, the people would ask a schoolteacher to preach and hold services for them. Twenty miles northwest of Philadelphia lived a little cluster of Reformed people at a place called Falkner Swamp. They asked John Philip Boehm to be their pastor. Two nearby churches also asked him to be their pastor. Boehm was a farmer, but he had been a schoolteacher in Germany. He was not yet ordained, but he agreed to serve these people. Boehm held his first communion service at Falkner Swamp on October 15, 1725, with about forty worshippers present. He drew up a constitution for his congregations, and the Reformed church in the United States was begun.

Other congregations soon sprang up in nearby places. They were small and weak. It was hard to get ministers. Boehm often had to visit distant churches to give communion, for there was no one else to do it. You can imagine that these trips were not easy, for there were no highways and automobiles. He died while making one such trip. We honor him as the father of the Reformed church.

The scattered congregations had no organization to tie them together. There were no regular meetings where their pastors and elders could come to know one another and lay plans together. The man who changed this was another pioneer, Michael Schlatter. He was Swiss but was sent to America by the Reformed church in Holland, which had taken an interest in the little Reformed congregations in the American wilderness. His purpose in coming was to gather these congregations together into one body. This he did in 1747 with the organization of the Coetus (pronounced "seetus" and meaning "coming together"). This was not a large body. At the first meeting in Philadelphia there were only four ministers and twenty-seven elders from twelve congregations. But the organization of this body was an important step in Reformed church history.

Schlatter traveled more than Boehm had done. He was pastor at Philadelphia, but he went into neighboring regions to meet Reformed people. Sometimes he found them so eager for the preaching of the gospel and for the Lord's Supper that they broke into tears when he stood before them. He also made a visit to Europe and raised sixty thousand dollars to aid these churches.

The Reformed Church Becomes Independent

The years rolled by. The Declaration of Independence was signed, and the thirteen colonies became a nation. The Reformed churches grew in number and membership. A college was begun at Lancaster, Pennsylvania, which was named for Benjamin Franklin. Just as the nation had become independent, so the young church decided to go on its own and separate from the Reformed church in Holland. In 1793 the first meeting of the Synod (assembly) of the German Reformed Church in the United States was held. The pioneer church had grown up and was now ready to ordain its own ministers and make its own decisions.

There were only thirteen ministers at this first synod meeting, but the new denomination did number 178 congregations and fifteen thousand members. These were scattered from New York to Virginia, with a few west of the Allegheny Mountains. In the years ahead, this church continued to grow. German Reformed people migrated into North Carolina, taking with them their faith. Reformed people also made their way across the mountains into Ohio and beyond. Later on, a strong colony settled in Wisconsin.

Widening And Deepening Church Life

Meanwhile the church was growing in other ways besides numbers. The first Sunday school in the Reformed church was started in First Church, Philadelphia, on April 14, 1806. A training school for ministers was badly needed, so a theological seminary was opened. To bind together all the various parts of the church, a church paper was started. One of the most important steps was the organization in 1838 of a Board of Foreign Missions. Through its work the message of Christ was spread to Japan, China, and Iraq.

Alongside the first synod in the East, another synod had been formed in Ohio with its own seminary, college, and church paper. The two synods were friendly, but they were separate. The several parts of the church now needed to be tied together more closely if they were to form a real church.

A great occasion was chosen for bringing them together—the three hundredth anniversary of the Heidelberg Catechism, which had been written in 1653. So in 1863, in the midst of the Civil War, the General Synod was organized. It met in Pittsburgh, on the border between the two synods.

The Reformed part of our church had now taken shape. There were many later changes, of course. The word German was dropped from the denominational name because most of the people were speaking English. New types of work were begun, and many new members were added as the years went by. After World War I, for example, about eighty Hungarian congregations, whose ties with the homeland were severed and whose support from Europe was cut off, came into organic connection with the Reformed church.

The Evangelical Part of Our Story

We must now go back some years and cross the ocean to Germany once more. There, both the Reformed and the Lutheran branches of the church had spread. King Frederick William III of Prussia wanted very much to bring the two together and have only one Protestant church. On the three hundredth anniversary of the Protestant Reformation, he gave an order uniting the two branches into the Evangelical Church of Prussia. (Evangel means "gospel," or "good news." The Evangelical church is, then, the church of the good news.) The union spread to other parts of Germany, so that there were thousands of people who held this Evangelical faith.

We are now thinking of a time two hundred years after the first Congregationalists and one hundred years after the first Reformed people came to America. Again the times were hard. Napoleon had all of Europe anxious. People endured war, poverty, and sickness. So, in the early 1800s, German people once more turned their eyes toward the new land of America. This time few of the German immigrants stayed along the East Coast, for the Midwest was opening up for settlement. The new immigrants either landed in the east and went west overland, or else they landed at New Orleans and went up the Mississippi River to St. Louis. These people brought their Evangelical faith with them, and they were the beginning of the Evangelical part of our story.

Beginnings In America

Among the readers of a book that spoke very highly of Missouri was a young man, well trained and well-to-do, by the name of Hermann Garlichs. He made his way to this country and settled about fifty miles west of St. Louis. There a little group of Evangelical people asked him to be their pastor, and in 1833 he organized the Femme Osage Church. In many ways he holds the place in the Evangelical part of our story that John Philip Boehm holds in the Reformed part. Like Boehm, he was not an ordained minister at the time. However, he agreed to serve the people because the need was so great. Like Boehm, he organized a first congregation, to be followed by many others. Like Boehm, he gave himself completely to his work. He organized seven congregations in the region, gave generously of his own money when a church building was needed, and even sacrificed his health for the work he loved.

Soon other congregations of the same sort sprang up, but each was separate from the rest. The man who brought them together was Louis E. Nollau. He did for the Evangelical part of our story what Michael Schlatter did for the Reformed part. Nollau came to America as a missionary, intending to go to the American Indians near the Pacific Coast. But while he and a companion missionary were waiting to set out from St. Louis into the Indian country, the companion took sick and died. This changed the course of Nollau's life. He became the pastor of a German Evangelical congregation at Gravois Settlement near St. Louis. Soon he saw the need for gathering together the separate churches of the region, and he sent out a letter to his fellow ministers, inviting them to his house to consider the matter. Six ministers, including Garlichs and Nollau, met in the log-cabin parsonage at Gravois Settlement, and there on October 15, 1840, they banded themselves together into the German Evangelical Church Society of the West. Two other pastors later joined these six. This society was not a synod. It was as yet only an association of pastors. But it was an important step in our history.

Pastor Nollau served the church in many ways. For a while he was a missionary in Africa. Later, when he was a pastor in St. Louis, he saw that the German people there needed medical care, and he started a hospital. He also began an orphanage during an epidemic. (Both of these institutions are still in existence and are rendering Christian service to the community.) Our church owes much to him.

The Society Becomes A Synod

In the years that followed, the Evangelical Church Society of the West grew in many ways. It started a theological seminary to train ministers. It began a church paper. It became much larger by including similar Evangelical organizations that had grown in Ohio and New York. During this time it gradually became much more than an association of ministers; it became a real church organization. So in 1866 it changed its name to the German Evangelical Synod of the West.

The man who was called to give all his time to this synod as its president was Pastor Adolf Baltzer. He had already served his church well. He had been president of a church college and, later, president and teacher in the theological seminary. Now, in addition to being president of the synod, he was for a while its treasurer, the editor of the church paper, and the superintendent of its publishing house. It is no wonder that he often had to work eighteen hours a day. Out of such devotion our church has come.

In due time there were other mergers with a synod reaching into northern Illinois and Wisconsin and with the Synod of the East. In 1877 the name was changed again—this time to the German Evangelical Synod of North America.

In 1884 the work was extended far beyond North America. In that year the Board of Foreign Missions was organized. It took over work already begun in India, and in 1920 it started a new missionary field in Honduras.

The Evangelical part of our church had now taken definite shape. It too dropped the word *German* in time and added new members and new lines of work as the years went by.

The Christian Part of Our Story

At the end of the eighteenth century and the beginning of the nineteenth, there were three outcroppings of religious dissent that were to have an important part in our story.

One was in Virginia, where James O'Kelly and thirty-one other ministers left the Methodist church in protest against the growing authority of its bishops. Their theory was that the Bible is a sufficient rule of faith and practice. Calling themselves the Christian church, they spread through many parts of the South.

Just after the turn of the nineteenth century, a group of dissenters in Vermont led by Dr. Abner Jones, a Baptist layman, revolted against the Calvinism of Congregationalists and Baptists. Independently, this group also took the name Christian. In 1808 Elias Smith founded the first religious newspaper in the United States, the *Herald of Gospel Liberty*, which became the official organ of the Christian church.

At the same time that this church came into being, a group of Presbyterians in Kentucky, led by the Reverend Barton W. Stone and the Reverend David Purviance, withdrew from the Presbyterian Synod of Kentucky. They, too, were disturbed by the rigidities of the Calvinism of the time and pleaded for more lay leadership, firmer reliance on the guidance of the Bible, and union with other followers of Christ. The Kentucky dissenters also called themselves *Christians.*

By 1808 these three groups were in contact with each other, and they informally agreed to work as one. For the name of their church they took the simple adjective *Christian,* which all three groups had chosen independently in the belief that followers of Christ should accept no sectarian labels. The first national meeting of the new denomination was held in Connecticut in 1820.

This church's view of its life and task was summarized in this bold statement: "The purpose of this church will be consummated in the reformation of the world and the union of all Christians."

The Christian church pioneered in educational opportunities for women, establishing several coeducational colleges. Like the Congregationalists, the Reformed church, and the Evangelical synod, Christians founded colleges to develop an educated clergy and laity. Their members were active in antislavery activities (as were the Congregationalists) and in missions overseas and on the frontiers.

Other Groups That Are Part of Our Story

We have already noted that Congregationalism began as a union of Pilgrims and Puritans in America. This happened in the early seventeenth century. There were few unions in the eighteenth century or during much of the nineteenth—these were times of westward expansion and the relating of church life to new frontiers. However, there were these unions:

1. The Congregational Methodist church, which was organized in Georgia in 1852 to secure a more democratic form of government than was afforded by the Methodist church of that day, grew in a generation through the neighboring states. In 1887 and 1888 about a third of this group united with the Congregational Churches.

2. In the early 1800s great numbers of German and Swiss people emigrated to America. Coming from Lutheran and Reformed communions, the majority went into churches of those denominations in this country, but many formed churches that were independent of any denomination whatever. Many of their leaders were distinguished for their breadth of thought and their concern for social justice. Eventually these churches united to form the Evangelical Protestant Church. In 1925 this church entered into union with the Congregational Churches.

3. Other Germans came to this country in the late 1800s from Russia, where they had lived for generations in German-speaking communities and had enjoyed their own congregationally organized churches. When in 1870 they were ordered to become Russians, many of them fled to America. Some of these people joined forces with the Congregational churches, while others joined the German Evangelical Synod of North America.

The Congregational Christian Churches

The emphasis and character of the Congregational churches and the Christian church led to conversations about the possibility of union. Both groups had similar origins and similar beliefs.

The Christians emphasized six principles:

1. The Lord Jesus Christ is the only head of the church.
2. The name *Christian,* to the exclusion of all party and sectarian names, is sufficient for the followers of Christ.
3. The Holy Scriptures, or the Scriptures of the Old and New Testaments, are the only creed, a sufficient rule of faith and practice.
4. Christian character, or vital Christian piety, is the only and sufficient test of Christian fellowship and church membership.
5. The right of private judgment and the liberty of conscience are a right and a privilege that should be accorded to and exercised by all.
6. The union of the followers of Christ should be pursued to the end that the world may believe.

Congregationalists put great stress on the covenant (agreement) that a church made in response to God's leading. A congregation was called a *covenant fellowship,* and those entering its membership were asked to "own the covenant" (to accept as their own the covenant that the church had declared). The covenant of the Salem, Massachusetts, church was adopted in 1629. Its words were as follows:

We covenant with the Lord and with one another and do bind our-selves in the presence of God to walk together in all [God's] ways, according as [God] is pleased to reveal [God's self] to us in [God's] blessed word of truth.

Congregationalists had adopted no creed as authoritative and binding, although creeds and affirmations of faith had significant place in Congregational churches. The spirit of Congregationalism was expressed in Pastor John Robinson's farewell in Holland to the departing Pilgrims: "God hath yet more light and truth to break forth from [God's] holy Word."

Because of the similarity of beliefs and practices, the union of the Congregationalists and Christians seemed natural, and the two denominations came together in 1931 as the Congregational Christian churches.

The Evangelical and Reformed Church

There was much in common between the Evangelical and the Reformed groups. The ancestors of both had come from Germany. Both had stood through the years for a well-educated ministry. Both shared in the Reformed tradition, although the Evangelical synod contained a stream of Lutheran influence also. Most important of all, both were thoroughly committed to cooperation and Christian fellowship with other denominations.

The two groups had dealings with one another in various ways. One of the six ministers who met at the Gravois Settlement in 1840 was a missionary of the Ohio synod of the Reformed church. For some years members of the two churches (together with others) joined in supporting the same Christian work in India. More than ten years before the union took place a respected minister of the Reformed church became a teacher in the theological seminary of the Evangelical Synod. Most important of all, the members of both were one in this—they had the same Lord.

It was only natural, therefore, that these two denominations should draw together. Their leaders drafted a Plan of Union, which was adopted by both groups. Then, on the evening of June 26, 1934, representatives of the two denominations gathered outside Zion Church in Cleveland, Ohio, and marched in together, two by two.

The former Reformed church was well known for its many institutions of learning, particularly its colleges, many of which have had a long history. This interest in educating young people in the Christian way of life as well as in academic studies extended even to the mission fields.

The former Evangelical synod was especially well known for its benevolent institutions. These included homes for the aged, homes for mentally disabled and epileptic people, hospitals, homes for children, city missions, and homes for retired ministers. This interest also extended to the mission fields.

Because both churches were greatly interested in foreign missions, the merger brought opportunities for more worldwide work. In addition to continuing work in the five countries where the two churches had been active, responsibility was assumed for two new fields: in Ecuador, South America, among the Andean Indians; and in West Africa, among the Ewe people.

One statement of the beliefs of the Evangelical and Reformed church was made in its constitution, as follows:

> The Holy Scriptures of the Old and New Testaments are recognized as the Word of God and the ultimate rule of Christian faith and practice.
>
> The doctrinal standards of the Evangelical and Reformed Church are the Heidelberg Catechism, Luther's Catechism, and the Augsburg Confession. They are accepted as an authoritative interpretation of the essential truth taught in the Holy Scriptures.
>
> Wherever these doctrinal standards differ, ministers, members, and congregations, in accordance with the liberty of conscience inherent in the gospel, are allowed to adhere to the interpretation of one of these confessions. However, in each case the final norm is the Word of God.
>
> In its relations to other Christian communions the Evangelical and Reformed Church shall constantly endeavor to promote the unity of the Spirit in the bond of peace.
>
> Congregations are allowed freedom of worship.

The United Church of Christ

On Tuesday, June 25, 1957, at Cleveland, Ohio, the Evangelical and Reformed church—twenty-three years old, passionate in its impulse to unity, committed to "liberty of conscience inherent in the Gospel"—and the Congregational Christian churches—twenty-six years old, a fellowship of biblical people under a mutual covenant for responsible freedom in Christ—joined together as the United Church of Christ. Two million members joined hands.

One might think that the differences in backgrounds and in methods of church government would make such a union difficult. The Congregational Christians trace their origin to England; the Evangelical and Reformed church is rooted in the Reformation in Germany and Switzerland. The Congregational Christians laid great stress on the autonomy of the local church; members of the Evangelical and Reformed church used the presbyterial type of government, which gives considerable power to synods and to the General Synod.

The youthful years of the United Church of Christ called the church to ministry in a society barely recovered from a war in Korea and soon thrust, with its burden of sorrow and guilt, into another in Vietnam. Burgeoning and expensive technologies in a shrinking world seemed to offer the bright prospect of ever more familiar human relationships, with fleeting promises of more time to enjoy them, yet generating ominous clouds of increasing crime, violence, and the fear of nuclear annihilation. The first years of the church's life occurred during a period of unprecedented national economic prosperity and hope, when, during the preceding decades, new church buildings had abounded to accommodate worshipers disinclined to consider their denomination important.

The priorities, pronouncements, and program recommendations of the General Synods throughout the 1960s and 1970s reflected a biblical sensitivity to God's care for a world that once led Jesus of Nazareth to weep over the city of Jerusalem. Concern for peace, ecumenism, and human rights grew in the United Church of Christ during the 1960s and into the 1970s with an increasingly louder voice. At the grass roots, many people worked for African American and other minority rights, for the elevation of women to equal regard and opportunity with men, for the just treatment and consideration of all persons of whatever sexual orientation, for a more humane criminal justice system, and for the enablement of people with handicaps to lead full lives.

At General Synod XIV the ministry sections of the constitution and bylaws were extensively amended; ministry to youths and young adults was adopted as a priority; a new Council on Racial and Ethnic Ministries was authorized; a mission partnership with the Presbyterian church of the Republic of Korea was approved; and such mission issues as a concern for people with AIDS, the establishment of justice and peace in Central America, and the evil of apartheid in South Africa received the careful attention of the delegates.

Delegates at General Synod XV, which met in Ames, Iowa, expressed their concern about the farm crisis in the United States, declared the United Church of Christ a Just Peace Church, supported sanctuary for political refugees escaping from South Africa and Central America, and supported full divestment of all financial resources from all corporations doing business with South Africa. In a historic action, General Synod XV voted for an ecumenical partnership with the Christian church (Disciples of Christ) and for a relationship with the Pentecostal church of Chile.

For the Class to Do

1.   Make a time line, using all the dates and events given in this chapter. Place this time line where the whole congregation can see it and get some idea of the history of our United Church of Christ.

2.   Make a poster for the church bulletin board showing the family tree of the United Church of Christ. (This tree would have roots and a trunk, but no branches!)

17

The Story of My Congregation

This story you must write yourself—with help from others. Some of the information you will need can be gathered from the record books of your church. Some of it you can get from your pastor, parents, church school teachers, members of the consistory or church council, and longtime members of the congregation. Some of it can be secured by visiting the various organizations in your church. It may be that you can find a booklet that was prepared for some special anniversary of the church, or you may find pictures of former buildings, old communion sets, or pulpit Bibles that come from years back in your church's history.

There is not room in this book to write out all that you might want to record about your own church. The questions in the following section suggest the kind of information you may want to include.

What to Find Out for Your Story

1. What is the full name of your congregation?
2. When was it begun? How old is it now?
3. How large is its membership?
4. Who were the charter members?
5. How did your congregation get started?
6. What interesting happenings have there been in the life of the congregation?
7. Who are some (or all) of the ministers and prominent members who have served the church during its history?
8. What is the name of the governing body of your church?

9. What committees do the work of the church?
10. How much is the church budget? How is it raised? How is it spent?
11. What outstanding acts of service has your church performed?
12. Have any ministers or missionaries come out of your church?
13. Who comprises the paid staff of your church? What work does each one do?
14. What are the chief organizations in your church?
15. When was your present church building built? If yours is an old congregation, find out about earlier buildings and locations.
16. What else does your church building contain besides the sanctuary? Does it have special rooms for education? for plays? for social events? What else?
17. Does your church have interesting art or stained-glass windows? What can you find out about them?
18. What can you find of interest on the outside of the building? Is there an inscription on the cornerstone? Is there a bell tower? a bell? bells? a carillon? Are there any old tombstones in the church's cemetery where founders of your church lie buried?
19. In what style of architecture is your church built?

Study the Church Sanctuary

Even though you attend the service of worship every Sunday, you have probably not seen everything there is to see in the sanctuary. Go there when no service is going on and examine every bit of furniture, every square foot of wall. You will probably be surprised to find many things that you had not noticed before. There may be things that you have wondered about. Why are they in the church? What are they used for?

As you enter the sanctuary, your eye may fall on the *communion table* or *altar*. From the earliest days of Christian history the bread and wine, which stand for the body and blood of Jesus, were placed on a communion table. As people thought about Jesus' death on the cross, they saw in it a sacrifice that could be compared to the sacrifices of animals offered on the altar in the Jewish temple—only much greater. Thus the church began to speak of the communion table as an altar. Since the Protestant Reformation many churches have used only the communion table because that is what the early church used. But whichever your church has, it should remind you of Jesus Christ our Savior.

The *pulpit* is the place where the minister stands when she or he preaches and brings God's word to the people.

The *baptismal font* is used to contain the water for baptism. The word *font* is much the same as "fountain."

Many churches have, in addition to the pulpit, a *lectern*. This comes from a Latin word meaning "to read." It is the stand from which the minister or others read the Bible in the service of worship.

Practically everything in the sanctuary has religious meaning of some sort and is placed there to help people worship God better. When an object stands for an idea, we call it a *symbol*. The communion table symbolizes Christ's communion with his followers. The pulpit and lectern symbolize the Word of God. The font symbolizes the water of baptism. See what other symbols you recognize in your church. Look on page 220 and see if you can find these symbols in your church. What Christian meaning do they have?

Does your church use altar coverings of different colors for different seasons of the church year? (See pages 216–217 for a list of the seasons.) If it does, the main colors are probably white, purple, green, and red, and each color symbolizes a Christian virtue. White represents new life and joy. Can you see why white is used on Christmas and Easter? Purple, or violet, represents penitence or humble sorrow for sin. Can you see why this color is used during Lent and Advent? Blue, the color of royalty and hope, may be used for Advent as we recall Christ's birth and await Christ's coming at the end of history. Green is the color of living things in nature. It is also the most ordinary color of all. It is all about us. Can you see why it is used during late spring and summer and early autumn? Red reminds us of fire and is the color associated with the Holy Spirit. It is used on Pentecost and at other Spirit-filled celebrations during the church year.

There are many other Christian symbols that you may find in your church. What do the following stand for?

A shepherd (John 10:11) _____

A lamb (John 1:29) _____

Lighted candles (John 8:12) _____

A cross (John 19:17–18)_____

An eye (Psalm 34:15) _____

A dove (Mark 1:10) _____

Tongues of fire (Acts 2:3–4) _____

A Community of Christians

A church is a Christian community, part of the great community of Christians around the earth. Its members are bound together with many close ties. When you are confirmed, you will become an adult member of this Christian community. As time goes on you will appreciate it more and more, and you will have many chances to do your part in it and for it. The more active you are, the more you will feel the closeness of the community.

Is there anything you as a class could do for your church now? Interview leaders in the church and your pastor to see what jobs there are in your church that people of your age can do.

18

The Church Service of Worship

O come, let us worship and bow down,
let us kneel before the Lord, our Maker!

For he is our God,
and we are the people of his pasture,
and the sheep of his hand.
                    —*Psalm 95:6-7*

How often we have heard these words as the minister opened the regular Sunday morning service of worship! They come to us out of our religious heritage, and they continue to call people to worship as they did back in the days of Hebrew worship in the temple.

The Weekly Miracle

Every Sunday, in big and little churches, in open country, village, and city, this kind of miracle takes place: People who are weary, confused, sad—bowed down with burdens of all kinds, tempted, fearful, and doubting—come to worship. During that time they lay their lives before God and listen to God speak. Hopefully, when they depart for their homes they are changed people. Hopefully, the burdens have been lifted, their fear is gone, and they can face life with new power and direction. Those who have come rejoicing go out with greater joy in God. Those who have been tempted receive strength to withstand temptation. Those who have been confused see the right way made clear. There is nothing more wonderful in all of life than this weekly miracle.

What Causes This Miracle?

God causes this miracle. God changes people. Anyone who turns to God and opens their life before God can be changed in just this way, for God is waiting for people to let God's Spirit come into their lives. The most glorious thing that can happen to us is to learn how to talk with God in true worship. We speak to God in prayer and hymn; God speaks to us through scripture and sermon and by connecting directly with our minds and hearts.

What Happens in Worship?

People who have given much thought and study to the experience of worship find that most of us are quite alike in what happens to us when we worship. Of course, we may have very brief, simple periods of worship that do not follow this kind of pattern. But when we give ourselves completely for a longer time of worship, we find that the following feelings come over us:

We think of God, how holy God is, how mighty God is, how good God is. We recall all that we know about God, and then have a feeling of how great God is—much greater than we can imagine. We call this point in our worship our vision of God. Some people call it *adoration*.

Next, our thoughts turn to ourselves. Having seen God's holiness, we see more sharply our own unholiness. When we see ourselves in God's light, we see our failures, our weaknesses, our sins. We know that we have not measured up to God's expectations for us. We are filled with humility, and we ask God to forgive us and let us start afresh. We call this point in our worship *repentance* or *confession*.

When we come humbly to God, sincerely asking God for forgiveness, God always forgives us our past sins and releases us from our old selves. This glorious feeling of being clean again must find expression in our thanking God. This is the point of *forgiveness* and *thanksgiving*.

We are now ready to hear what God's will is for our lives. God has a message for us, and we are listening and waiting for it. Some call this point of worship *illumination*, for now we see clearly what God wants us to do. Most of us call it *communion*.

We accept God's challenge. We promise to be true to the new light God has given us. This is our dedication, our acceptance of God's will.

An Old Testament Experience of Worship

One of the finest examples of worship is described in highly poetic language in Isaiah 6:1-8. Isaiah was a young man when King Uzziah died. The old monarch had ruled for a long time, and he had been a good ruler. The whole nation had come to depend greatly on him. His son was a poor person to take his place. So when King Uzziah died, there was a feeling of helplessness and confusion and unrest. Furthermore, the powerful nation of Assyria was threatening the land. With a feeling of fear and concern, Isaiah went to the temple to worship. It was then that he had the experience about which he writes in chapter 6 of his book. Read his words thoughtfully.

Isaiah in the Temple   The Order of Worship

1. We Turn Our Thoughts Toward God

I saw the Lord, high and lifted up.
"Holy, holy, holy is the Lord of hosts; the whole earth is full of his glory."

Prelude (music that helps us to turn our thoughts toward to God.)

Opening Sentence—In the name of the triune God: the Creator, the Christ, and the Holy Spirit. Or—The grace of our Lord Jesus Christ, the love of God, and the communion of the Holy Spirit be with you all.

2. We Feel Our Unworthiness And God's Forgiveness

"Woe is me! for I am lost; for I am a [person] of unclean lips."
"Your guilt is taken away, and your sin is forgiven."

Confession of Sin—Most merciful god, we confess that we are in bondage to sin and cannot free ourselves.

Assurance of Pardon—Friends, believe the good news of the gospel; in Jesus Christ, we are forgiven.

3. We Praise God and Learn God's Will for Our Lives

And I heard the the voice of the Lord saying, "Whom shall I send, and who will go for us"

A Hymn of Praise.

Reading of Scripture (including the Old Testament, Epistle, and Gospel).

Sermon (in which the minister reflects with us on the Scripture).

Affirmation of Faith (the Statement of Faith of the United Church of Christ, a creed, or a church covenant).

Hymn.

4. We Give Ourselves To God's Will And Care

Then I said, "Here I am! Send me."

Prayers of the People—(including thanksgiving and intercession).

The Lord's Prayer.

Offertory (in which we offer our money and our ourselves for the service of God in the world).

Doxology (or a hymn of consecration).

Holy Communion (we are fed for discipleship)

Hymn.

Commissioning and Benediction—The grace of our Lord Jesus Christ, the love of God, and the communion of the Holy Spirit be with you all.

Postlude (music to send us out).

The Order of Worship for the Sunday Morning Service

One way of understanding an order of worship is to look at it alongside the experience that Isaiah had. Note how this was done on pages 136–137. The two columns are not entirely alike, as you will see, but they are enough alike for our purpose, which is to find a helpful way of thinking about the order of worship as you experience it in your church.

Compare this order of worship with the one used in your congregation. It may be the same, or it may be quite different. Our churches are free to use whatever form they wish. The point to remember is that there is an order of worship, and if you examine the service used in your church you will find that it will most probably include the four main parts indicated on pages 136–137. It may be that a hymn like "Holy, Holy, Holy, Lord God Almighty" will turn your thoughts to God. There may be an invocation (a prayer calling on God and the Holy Spirit), such as that fine one that begins "Almighty God, unto whom all hearts are open, all desires know, and from whom no secrets are hid; cleanse the thoughts of our hearts by the inspiration of your Holy Spirit." In words such as these you are led to feel your unworthiness and are made ready to receive God's forgiveness.

Study your church's order of worship and think about each part. See if you understand why the parts come in the order they do. If there are any parts of the service that you do not understand, ask your pastor to explain them to you so that you can participate most meaningfully in the services of worship.

How to Enter into Worship Fully

Understanding the order of worship being used is important if you are to worship fully. But this is not enough. Turn back to page 2 and reread "Going to Church." Then ask yourself questions like the following:

Can I really worship God on Sunday if I have not thought of God during the week? Why or why not?

Can I quarrel with my family from eight to nine on Sunday morning and then worship God well from eleven to twelve? Why or why not?

Why do people want to worship God? Because of God's great goodness? Because God wants them to? Because they are made stronger and better by being in his presence?

The writer of Psalm 42 said,

> *My soul thirsts for God,*
> *for the living God.*
> *When shall I come and behold*
> *the face of God?*

Do I feel that way about worship at church? Should I?

Your Church's Service of Worship

On Sunday, notice the different parts of the service, how they follow one another. Try to see why each part is included. For instance, how does the prelude help people to worship God? What purpose does the anthem serve? Then write the information asked for below.

The Parts of The Service   **The Central Thought Of Each**

What part of the service of worship do you like the most? _____

_____

_____

_____

Why do you like·it?

Components of Worship

How do the following aid you to worship God?

Prayer _____

Hymns Music _____

Sermon Offering _____

Bible Reading _____

Architecture _____

Art _____

Stained-Glass Windows _____

Symbols _____

Appropriate Hymns

Select a hymn from your hymnal that is appropriate for each of the following themes:

Thanksgiving _____

Love _____

Faith _____

Joy _____

Praise _____

Prayer _____

Consecration _____

Confirmation _____

Baptism _____

The Lord's Supper _____

Palm Sunday _____

Easter _____

Christmas _____

Missions _____

Pentecost _____

19

The Sacraments

Do you remember being baptized? If you were baptized as an infant or a young child, you probably do not remember. If you were baptized as an older child or will be baptized before you are confirmed, you will remember. But even if you don't remember your own baptism, you might have seen others baptized. Usually this takes place in front of the congregation during a Sunday morning service. If the baptism is for an infant or a young child, the minister asks the parents or guardians several questions. If older children or adults are being baptized, the minister will ask them the questions. But no matter who it is, the minister prays, says the person's name, and then puts water three times on the person's head. Why does the minister do this? Why the water? Why three times? What does it mean? Some people think baptism is just a way of giving a baby a name. Is that all it is? For Christians, baptism is a sacrament. What is a sacrament?

Doubtless you have been in church when the Lord's Supper was being observed. You have noticed that the service is somewhat different from the usual order of worship. The people are especially reverent that Sunday. At a given point, all take bread and eat it and then drink from a cup or small glass. Why do they do this? Why the bread and wine? Why are the people especially reverent? If members of the church are ill, the pastor or deacons will give them communion in their homes. Why do they do this? We also speak of the Lord's Supper as a sacrament. What is a sacrament?

What We Mean by Sacrament

To begin with, the word *sacrament* originally meant "something sacred." You can see that it is much the same as *sacred* and *consecrate*. It was the sacred vow that a Roman soldier took when joining the army. It was the money deposited in a sacred place beforehand by the two parties in a lawsuit. It was a sacred ceremony in a certain religion of the Roman world. In time, Christians used it when they spoke of what was sacred to them. Bernard of Clairvaux, the monk who called Christians to set out on the Second Crusade, spoke of ten sacraments. Another church leader who lived about the same time mentioned only five. The Roman Catholic church today speaks of seven sacraments. We in our own denomination, along with most other Protestants, speak of only two—baptism and the Lord's Supper. They are truly sacred to us.

These two sacraments have been in the church from the very beginning. About A.D. 150 a man named Justin Martyr wrote about baptism and the Lord's Supper in his day. As you read the following, remember that it was written over eighteen hundred years ago:

> As many as are persuaded and believe that the things are true which are taught and said by us, and promise that they are able to live accordingly, they are taught to pray and with fasting to ask God for forgiveness of their former sins, while we pray and fast with them. Thereupon they are brought to us to where there is water, and are born again in the same manner of a new birth as we, also, ourselves were born again. For in the name of God the Father and Lord of all, and of our Savior Jesus Christ, and of the Holy Spirit, they then receive the washing in the water.
>
> And on the day called the Day of the Sun there is a gathering in one place of us all who live in cities or in the country, and the memoirs of the apostles or the writings of the prophets are read as long as time allows. Then, when the reader has ceased, the president gives by word of mouth his admonition and exhortation to imitate these excellent things. Afterward we all rise at once and offer prayers; and as I said, when we have ceased to pray, bread is brought and wine and water, and the president likewise offers up prayers and thanksgiving as he has the ability, and the people assent, saying "Amen." The distribution to each and the partaking of that for which thanks were given then take place; and to those not present a portion is sent by the hands of the deacons.[1]

So you can see that both of these sacraments are sacred with age. Our forbearers have used them for many, many years.

The Sacraments Were Instituted by Jesus

Both baptism and the Lord's Supper go back to Jesus himself—what he did as well as what he said.

Remember how, when Jesus left the carpenter shop in Nazareth, he went into the river Jordan and was baptized by John. This was the beginning of his ministry. It was then that he consecrated himself wholly to God's will and that he felt surer than ever before of his nearness to God. After he had gone, members of the early church remembered him as saying to them: "Go therefore and make disciples of all nations, baptizing them in the name of the Father and of the Son and of the Holy Spirit" (Matthew 28:19).

You know also how, on Thursday evening of that last week of Jesus' life, just before his arrest, he and his disciples gathered in an upper room for a last supper together. This is a scene that Christians have never forgotten and never want to forget. Every time we observe the Lord's Supper we call this scene to mind. Jesus began this observance and he told us to keep it up through the years, saying: "Do this in remembrance of me" (Luke 22:19).

Symbolic Acts

Both baptism and the Lord's Supper are symbolic acts. That is, they stand for something spiritual. In both sacraments there is something that we see and something that we do not see.

In *baptism* we see the water that is used. But there is much that we do not see. In adult baptism, we do not see the repentance and the consecration of the adult person who is being baptized. In infant baptism we do not see the hopes and dreams and plans of the parents or guardians as they bring their baby to God and the church. We do not see the entire Christian church of which the child or individual is becoming a member, for it goes around the world and back through the ages. We do not see God's gracious love reaching out to forgive the sins of the individual.

In the *Lord's Supper* we see the bread and wine (or grape juice) that are used. But again there is much that we do not see. We do not see the many hearts whose cares and worries grow less as God's love in Jesus becomes real to them in the breaking of the bread. Nor do we see the many hearts in which new resolutions are being made to follow Jesus wherever he would have them go. Nor do we see the countless souls around the world and in the life beyond who have also eaten of the Lord's Supper and may almost be thought of as sitting down with us at this sacred meal. We do not see the spirit of Jesus himself. We do not see God's gracious love continually seeking us out to make and keep us pure—the love that was made so clear to people when our Lord's body was broken and his blood shed on the cross.

We shall not be far wrong, then, if we think of a sacrament as a sacred observance coming from Jesus himself and combining something seen with something unseen.

What Baptism Means

In Holy Baptism God imparts the gift of the new life unto people, receives them into fellowship as God's children, and admits them as members of the Christian church.

Look back over this paraphrase from answer 118 in the Evangelical Catechism and notice the three parties involved in baptism—God, people, the church. When the people being baptized confess their faith in Christ and resolve to give up whatever is evil in their life, then God through the Holy Spirit opens the way into a new and better life, the Christian way of life. This Christian way takes place in the church, and it is through a minister of the church of Jesus Christ that the new Christians are received into this great community. So often, as we witness a baptism, we think only of the visible participants—the candidates for baptism and the minister. But unless God is active in the process, it is not complete, it is not sacred, it is not a sacrament.

In infant baptism, the baby being baptized is dedicated to the Lord by parents (or guardians) and sponsors, and God receives the child into God's realm through the ministries of a Christian pastor. In one order for the baptism of infants we find these words, to be spoken by the minister:

> The sacrament of baptism is an outward and visible sign of the grace of God. Inasmuch as the promise of the gospel is not only to us but also to our children, baptism with water and the Holy Spirit is the mark of their acceptance into the care of Christ's church, the sign and seal of their participation in God's forgiveness, and the beginning of their growth into full Christian faith and discipleship. [2]

Church Practices in Baptism

The church uses water in baptism to represent the inner cleansing of a person's life. Just as his or her body is made clean with water, so he or she is to become clean within as he or she begins the new life of a Christian. Read Ezekiel 36:25–27 and see how, even in Old Testament times, water had this meaning. John the Baptist, of course, is best known for practicing baptism to help prepare the way for the coming of the Savior. The Christian church has also used the symbolism of water in baptism throughout the centuries.

In our church it is usually the custom to sprinkle a few drops of water on the head of the person being baptized. In some of our churches and in other denominations, the person goes down into a stream or a baptismal tank in the church until he or she is completely covered. Do you think it makes any difference how much water is used? Why?

Why does the minister place water three times on the head of the person who is joining the church? (See Matthew 28:19.)

When adults are baptized, they are asked to confess their faith to join the community of Christians. When infants are baptized, parents, guardians, sponsors, and the congregation are asked to make a number of promises on behalf of the child. This baptism takes place with the expectation that the children will later accept the faith into which they were baptized and will take upon themselves the responsibilities of membership in the Christian church.

What are the promises made by the parents, guardians, sponsors, and congregation? What do you suppose faithful parents or guardians think while their child is being baptized? What are they hoping? Why must one or both parents or guardians be members of the church to have their baby baptized? What is the responsibility of the sponsors? What is the role of the congregation?

In some churches the baptismal font is placed inside the main entrance. Baptism is a sign of entrance into the Christian church; therefore, to have the baptism occur at the door of the church makes the act even more symbolic. Most of our churches have it in front, in full view of the worshiping congregation. What is the symbolism of this?

What the Lord's Supper Means

Answers 126 and 127 in the Evangelical Catechism tells us the following about the Lord's Supper:

> The Lord's Supper is the sacrament by which we receive the body and blood of our Lord Jesus Christ as the nourishment of our new life, strengthen the fellowship with Christ and all believers, and confess that he has died for us. As we eat and drink in the Lord's Supper we receive forgiveness of sins, life, and salvation. For so it is written: Broken and shed for you for the remission of sins. We receive the blessings of the Lord's Supper only as we eat and drink with heartfelt repentance and true faith in our Lord Jesus Christ.

You will want to read for yourself the oldest account we have of how the Lord's Supper was begun (see 1 Corinthians 11:23–26). This event took place the night before Jesus was crucified (when his body was broken and his blood was shed on the cross). Ever since that time, the bread and the wine have recalled for Christians Jesus' death on the cross. There his love for people, and also God's love for people, was shown most clearly. Can you see why many people feel closer to Jesus and to God in the Lord's Supper than at any other time?

When we eat the bread and take the cup, we are to remember Jesus. What should we remember about him? His life? His teachings? His death? His goodness? Our faith that he is alive today?

Sometimes the Lord's Supper is called the Eucharist. In some orders for Holy Communion you will find a Eucharistic Prayer. The word *Eucharist* comes from a Greek word meaning "thanksgiving." For what should we be especially thankful in the communion service?

We have seen how natural it is to feel our nearness to Jesus and to God in this service. Are there any others with whom we might feel a close sense of community, communion? What about the other Christians in the sanctuary who are joining with us in this solemn observance? What about other Christians in America and Europe and Asia and Africa and Australia who at the same moment or at other times join in this observance? What about those who have gone before us, the women and men of faith in every age?

Chalice

Baptismal Font

Should there be any difference in our lives after we take part in this service? Should we try to make a difference? What difference? A closing prayer that is used in some orders of Holy Communion does two things: (1) it offers thanks to God for God's great goodness, and (2) it prays that God may assist the worshipers with grace so that they may continue in holy community and may do all such good works as are pleasing to God.

Some churches use wine, and others use unfermented grape juice. Some use bread, and others use bread made without yeast and formed into thin, round wafers. Do you think it makes any difference which are used? Why?

When you have taken communion, you will afterwards have time for quiet thought and prayer. What prayer might you offer at this time? Write in the space below a prayer that you could use.

The Christian Sacraments

1. What is a sacrament?

2. What are the sacraments of our church?

3. Why do we have these sacraments?

4. What do we mean when we say that the sacraments are symbolic acts?

5. Who administers the sacraments?

The Sacraments

I. Baptism

1. What happens in baptism?

2. What three parties are involved in baptism?
   a. _____
   b. _____
   c. _____

3. What symbol is used in baptism? _____

4. Where do we find the words of institution of this sacrament?

5. What responsibilities rest on those who have been baptized?

6. What is the promise given to us in baptism? (See Acts 2:38-39.)

7. Give a definition of *baptism* in your own words.

8. Why does our denomination practice infant baptism as well as adult baptism?

II. The Lord's Supper

1. What is the Lord's Supper?

2. Why do we speak of the Lord's Supper as *communion?*

3. The two elements used in the Lord's Supper are:
   a. _____
   b. _____

4. Of what is the bread a symbol? _____

5. Of what is the wine a symbol?_____

6. How can you prepare yourself to receive the Lord's Supper worthily?

7. In what way is the Lord's Supper a sign of God's love?

8. What benefits do we receive from the Lord's Supper?

9. What responsibilities rest on a Christian after he or she has partaken of the supper?

10. About what or whom should you be thinking as you receive the elements?

11. Look in your hymnal and find two communion hymns. Write their titles here.
    a. _____
    b_____

12. How often should a Christian come to the Lord's Table?

PART FIVE
Christianity in Action

20
The Work Our Denomination Is Doing

There are many things that neither you nor your congregation could do alone. You could not start a college and support it. You could not build a hospital or start a major urban mission. It would be hard for you to send one or more missionaries to other countries and support them. There are a variety of tasks related to God's work that can best be done by a number of churches working together as a denomination in mission.

How Our Denomination Is Organized

The United Church of Christ is one of the major American Protestant denominations. Its membership is approximately 1,302,308. These members live in almost every state and in the District of Columbia. In addition, there are churches of our denomination in Canada and Puerto Rico. Because all these people cannot gather together in one place to legislate action and plan for the future, a representative organization is a practical necessity. The United Church of Christ works through local churches, associations, conferences, the General Synod, and covenanted, affiliated and associate ministries.

The 1,302,308 members of the United Church of Christ are gathered into about 5,804 local *congregations*. These congregations are grouped into thirty-nine *conferences* that, in most instances, are formed along state lines. In the case of a state like Pennsylvania where there are many churches, it is desirable to have several conferences. In sparsely settled sections of the nation or where there are few United Church of Christ congregations, a conference consists of more than one state. Conferences are organizations that provide mutual strength, develop common programs, and address state-level concerns. Your minister can tell you about the conference to which your church belongs and what its boundaries and programs are.

Conferences are divided into *associations,* which are smaller groups of churches that unite for community and for carrying out the work of the church in a particular geographical area.

Once every two years, delegates elected from each of the thirty-nine conferences and members of the boards of directors of the *covenanted ministries* come together in a *General Synod.* The General Synod is something like Congress, except that it meets less frequently and its actions are not binding on the member churches. The General Synod approves the budget of the United Church of Christ and nominates and elects the officers of the church, the directors of the covenanted ministries, and the Executive Council. It maintains the treasury for the church, determines ecumenical relationships, and with the participation of the conferences, adopts and amends the constitution and by-laws of the church.

The pastor of the United Church of Christ is called the general minister and president. Other officers are the associate general minister and the executive ministers of the three programmatic covenanted ministries. These five persons are elected to this full-time work for a four-year term and make up the *collegium* of officers of the church.

An *Executive Council* is elected by the General Synod to carry on its work between meetings and to give more sustained attention to matters of United Church of Christ policy and program. The seventy or more members of the Executive Council are clergy and lay people.

Major administrative and program work of the denomination is done through four agencies. They are called *covenanted ministries* because they minister or serve on behalf of the church and of Jesus Christ in a close relationship with one another. Their names are as follows:

Office of General Ministries
Wider Church Ministries
Justice and Witness Ministries
Local Church Ministries

There are also two other ministries whose executive ministers are not elected by General Synod. One is an affiliated ministry called the Pension Boards of the United Church of Christ. The other is an associated ministry called the United Church Foundation. In addition, the General Synod approved diverse organizations to do specialized work. Among them are:

Council on Ecumenism
Historical Council
Council on Higher Education
Council of Theological Education
Council for Racial and Ethnic Ministries

Look in the *Yearbook* of the United Church of Christ and find the names of the officers of the denomination as well as the staff and members of the various covenanted ministries and committees.

How do church members know what the denomination is doing? Two publications provide communication links: *United Church News* and an *Annual Report*. Most conferences have a newsletter or paper to interpret the work of the United Church of Christ in a given region. The *Calvin Synod Herald* performs this function for the Calvin Synod conference, whose members are of Hungarian background.

In these publications are articles that tell what churches are doing and that deal with issues of importance to members of the United Church of Christ. They also include reports on the work of conferences, covenanted ministries, and the General Synod. Such publications help to link all the churches and members together. Additionally, the denomination's website, www.ucc.org, offers an abundance of information and links to bodies related to the United Church of Christ.

The Work Our Denomination Is Doing

Office of General Ministries

The Office of General Ministries (OGM) cares for the spiritual life, unity and well-being of the church, coordinates the planning of General Synod and the implementation of the actions of General Synod. It nurtures the church's covenantal life and its ecumenical and interfaith relationships, provides processes for theological reflection and the visioning, planning and coordination of the work of the national setting of the church. It manages shared support services necessary for the effective operation of the all the covenanted ministries. The work of this ministry is organized in four major areas in addition to the overall pastoral work of the general minister and president.

Still Speaking Initiative Ministry is a new expression of the commitment of the United Church of Christ to tell more clearly its story of being a multiracial, multicultural, open and affirming church accessible to all. This ministry, through the use of creative ads on commercial television and in newspapers, is making the public more aware of what the denomination intends by its passion to be a church inclusive of all who seek a saving relationship with God.

Common Services Ministry provides resources for community life within *Church House,* affirmative action and diversity initiatives, archival functions and the work of a parish nurse. It also offers the services of specialists in human resources (personnel), financial management, meeting planning, research functions that include the publication of the *Yearbook,* information systems technology and central services that involve photocopying and a large range of other support work.

Covenantal Relations Ministry focuses on means to honor the ecumenical vocation of the church and its participation in the World and National Councils of Churches, the World Alliance of Reformed Churches and Churches Uniting in Christ. It implements the commitment of the national setting to stand in solidarity with the conferences of the denomination and to embrace the concerns of the racial and ethnic constituencies of the United Church of Christ.

Proclamation, Identity, and Communication Ministry is a center for publishing *United Church News,* creating special interpretive literature and audiovisuals, preparing public news releases, designing and managing the website of the denomination and advocating fairness in the media of the nation.

Financial Development Ministry addresses both the short and long term challenge of the church to identify and relate to those who wish to support the denomination's work through immediate or planned gifts, including bequests from estates and wills, and grants from foundations

Wider Church Ministries

Wider Church Ministries (WCM) represents the United Church of Christ in mission beyond the borders of the United States and in disaster ministries at home and abroad. Its mandate is to demonstrate in practical ways the church's conviction that God cares for all people everywhere. Its purpose is to encourage and support all settings of the denomination to participate in the global church and to conduct common global ministries with the Christian Church (Disciples of Christ). With all the Covenanted Ministries, it is committed to an inclusive, multiracial, multicultural, open and affirming church accessible to all. Its work is clustered in four geographical regions: Africa, Latin American and the Caribbean, the Middle East and Europe, and Southern Asia.

In a world of many faiths and beliefs, since 1810 the WCM has enabled Christians to cross the boundaries of language, culture, nation, and race to share the gospel. Today, UCC missionaries serve by invitation as mission partners in foreign countries to aid in *Global Education and Advocacy* through:

- strengthening local congregations by sharing specialized personnel and program support;
- providing leadership training for lay people and clergy;
- supporting cooperative health services, including family planning, preventative medicine, community health education, and local delivery of health care;
- assisting local development, rural and urban, through appropriate technology, agricultural skills, and vocational training;
- supporting education by preparing young people for the challenges of the future by introducing Christian values and global sensitivities;
- addressing United States public policy and educating UCC members and others as to the impact that government and corporate practices have on people around the world; and
- sharing diverse expressions of worship, faith, witness, and service by providing opportunities for people and churches to have contact through visits and special relationships.

Additionally, WCM provides means for the *Global Sharing of Resources* through:

- the recruitment and placement of volunteers in service to human need both at home and abroad;
- a national disaster ministry program that addresses suffering as a consequence of disasters anywhere in our land and provides volunteers for needed services; and
- a refugee sponsorship and resettlement program.

A *Health and Wholeness Advocacy Ministry* is also lodged in WCM for the purpose of nurturing the partnership of all settings of the denomination with the health and welfare institutions related to the United Church of Christ and to provide a focus on gay, lesbian, bisexual and transgender concerns and HIV/AIDS ministries.

Justice and Witness Ministries

The purpose of Justice and Witness Ministries (JWM) is to enable and encourage local churches, associations, conferences and national expressions of the United Church of Christ to engage in God's mission globally by direct action for the integrity of creation, justice and peace.

It seeks to fulfill its responsibilities through four ministry teams, deployed staff at the Franklinton Center at Bricks (North Carolina), a Washington, D.C. office and regional desks for a Justice and Peace Action Network.

Economic Justice Ministry addresses concerns related to poverty and its causes in a world where resources are not justly shared, suffering prevails in the midst of affluence and the environment is harmed by patterns of waste and over-consumption. It seeks to alert society to the health and wellness needs of all persons, the rights and responsibilities of laborers and those who employ them, and the important place of quality public education in the heritage of our nation.

Human Rights, Justice for Women, and Transformation Ministry focuses on cherished protections of human rights in a democracy that holds sacred the conscience and freedom of all its citizens. It provides advocacy for penal reform and the transformation of our criminal justice system, for the best interests of children and families and for struggles related to human sexuality. It labors for a transformation of human hearts that will enable us to welcome more fully a church and society committed to the multiracial and multicultural inclusion of all persons. It continues the prophetic witness of our denomination to full regard for women as equal partners with men in the exercise of their gifts, rights and roles of leadership.

Racial Justice Ministry addresses the impact of the sin of racism historically and in our midst today. It continues the heritage of our church's involvement in the *Amistad* incident of 1839, the abolitionist movement of that century and the civil rights movement of the twentieth century. It provides resources for antiracism training, conflict resolution, empowerment of youth and young adults of color, and education for environmental justice, especially as it relates to toxic pollution in areas populated by the poor, the elderly and persons of color. Through the Franklinton Center, rooted in the African American heritage of our church, it seeks to promote justice for rural farm communities and offers educational conferences for persons of all ages and races.

Public Life and Social Policy Ministry offers assistance to all settings of the church in the implementation of actions of the General Synod and other church bodies related to social and governmental issues. It invites broad participation of members of the church in these issues through the Justice and Peace Action Network. Through the Washington office, this ministry interfaces with members of congress, the federal courts and the White House. It cooperates with other faith communities to achieve positive change in areas as diverse as full rights for persons with disabilities, tax reform, health care, immigration law, the repeal of capital punishment, sound environmental policy and many other matters.

Local Church Ministries

The mission of Local Church Ministries (LCM) is to serve God in the United States and Puerto Rico by doing what the church has always been called to do: declare God's love for all people and demonstrate the fruits of that love. Local Church Ministries assists local churches and the wider life of the United Church of Christ to respond in creative and contemporary ways to five centers to action.

Parish Life and Leadership Ministry assists local churches in their search process for pastors and provides resources concerning church vocations, scholarships and authorization for commissioned, licensed and ordained ministry. It maintains background information on each United Church of Christ minister so that a church that needs a pastor can learn about potential candidates. It works closely with the denomination's theological seminaries and provides scholarship help for theological students. It also supports specialized ministries, such as chaplains in the military, in hospitals, and in prisons.

In addition, the agency develops lay-training programs through which laity can participate more fully in the church's life. Through its support of professional leadership and resources like the United Church of Christ Manual on Ministry, it assists local churches, associations and conferences in fulfilling their ministry.

Evangelism Ministry supports congregations in their efforts to hear and respond to Gods call and to strengthen their growth and outreach. It is responsible for sharing the good news of the Christian message. The local congregation is the focus of this Ministry's work. People and program resources assist in embracing evangelism, achieving membership growth, increasing worship attendance, and enhancing spiritual life.

Through partnership with conferences, this Ministry supports the development of new churches, revitalizes other churches, subsidizes and trains pastors of all churches, and provides funds to purchase property. This division also provides loans to help congregations build new facilities and renovate older ones.

Publication, Resources and Distribution Ministry creates, markets and distributes curricula, books and other products through Pilgrim Press and United Church Press. It provides resources for denominational, ecumenical, academic and general use. It collaborates with all the covenanted ministries, through its design and production department, to create printed resources that support their work. Its program resources include Bibles, hymnals, confirmation materials, and camp and Conference publications.

This Ministry manages United Church of Christ Resources, a warehouse and distribution center, which provides services for all the covenanted, associated and affiliated ministries of the denomination as they seek to serve local churches. The staff maintains an inventory of all items listed in the several catalogues of the church and is responsible for shipping all materials to those who order them.

Stewardship and Church Finances Ministry invites and nurtures people to be stewards of and in all of life, giving of time, self, and wealth. It provides leadership, printed and audiovisual resources, and educational programs to assist members and local churches in understanding and practicing what it means to be responsible stewards of God's creation.

This Ministry carries out its responsibilities through three services. First, stewardship education is encouraged through resources like *Inspiring Generosity* and a Stewardship Associate initiative program to train dispersed leadership throughout the conferences. Second, mission interpretation that includes a video presentation of the need for and use of the offerings promoted by the General Synod. And third, through the promotion of Our Church's Wider Mission (OCWM), including Basic Support. This requires the preparation of stewardship theme material, weekly Mission Moments, the Sunday Bulletin Service, and the *United Church of Christ Desk Calendar and*

Plan Book, as well as work with pastors and seminaries to encourage steward-ship growth in local churches.

Among the Ministry's publications, productions, and programs are:
- the *United Church of Christ Desk Calendar and Plan Book*
- the *United Church of Christ Sunday Bulletins* and the
  Stewardship Messages for UCC Weekly Offering Envelopes;
- *Inspiring Generosity*—the basic resources for local churches;
- *Take Hold of Real Life*—a DVD resource for all ages;
- God's Gift, My Gifts—a resource created for
  children but with broad appeal;
- *Mission Moments*—brief stories to connect congregations
- *Our Church's Wider Mission Brochure*—a description of how
  mission is funded; and
- the four annual all-church offerings—
  One Great Hour of Sharing—Giving Help, Hope and Life
  Neighbors in Need—Justice and Compassion Like a Mighty Stream
  The Christmas Fund—Remembering Those Who
  Serve the Church, and
  Strengthen the Church—Faithfully Building the Body of Christ

The education of church members to be stewards of all of life; the strengthening of congregations for mission locally, nationally, and globally; and the large-scale increase of church and mission support are among the top priorities of Stewardship and Church Finances Ministry in its work with the members and congregations of the United Church of Christ.

Worship and Education: encourages and supports the development and use of resources for all ages and settings of life that enrich the vitality of worship and the educational experiences of local churches and other ministry settings, including places of higher education. Among its publications are *Worship Ways, Common Lot,* the *Mosaic Series,* curricula, confirmation mate-rials and new editions of the *Book of Worship.* Contemporary worship materi-als, including those published in Spanish, are regularly posted on the website, www.ucc.org.

It also relates to the Council for Higher Education and the Council of Presidents of our six historic African American colleges founded by the American Missionary Association. It provides staff support for the work of the Council of Youth and Young Adult Ministries and is responsible for the administration of the National Youth Event. It supports the National Musicians Network of the denomination and continues the educational work of the Coordinating Center for Women.

The Pension Boards
(An Affiliated Ministry of the United Church of Christ)

The Pension Boards provide employee benefit programs, including health and dental insurance, designed to assist ministers and lay workers in achieving financial security. They oversee retirement benefits, disability and life insurance, the Christmas Fund Appeal, and the United Church Board for Ministerial Assistance.

The United Church Foundation
(An Associated Ministry of the United Church of Christ)

The United Church Foundation provides a means by which individuals and organizations of the United Church of Christ may exercise their stewardship of resources through the investment of funds for the sake of strengthening the mission entrusted to the church.

Under-represented Groups and Constituencies

As you review the United Church of Christ's story, you will be aware of the many different groups represented in its life. The United Church of Christ is a union of different traditions, people, styles, and interests. Historically under-represented groups are increasingly important in the UCC's life. Among them are the United Church of Christ Coalition for Lesbian, Gay, Bisexual and Transgender Concerns, the National Committee on Disabilities and the Council for Youth and Young Adult Ministries. They are represented on the Executive Council. Organizations that represent the historic racial and ethnic constituencies of our denomination are also represented on the Executive Council and relate to the Office of General Ministries.

In 1966 a group of African American ministers joined together with an interest to organize African American lay people within the United Church of Christ. This group successfully established themselves as Ministers for Racial and Social Justice (MRSJ). Today, because of their focus to close the widening economic gap, it is known as Ministers for Racial, Economic, and Social Justice (MRSEJ). Out of this group developed the United Black Churchmen, today known as the United Black Christians (UBC). This organization, which includes African American lay people, clergy and youth within the UCC, represents the African American constituency within the larger church.

The Council for American Indian Ministries (CAIM) is responsible for ministry in partnership with the native American constituency of the UCC. Among its many responsibilities is to end negative stereotyping of American Indians in the media, textbooks, and sports. Its work is supported by the Neighbors in Need Offering.

In 1975, the Pacific Islander and Asian American Ministries (PAAM) was formed to provide representation for Chinese, Japanese, Filipino, Samoan, Hawaiian, Korean, and Southeast Asian people, including Christians from India, within the UCC.

The Council for Hispanic Ministries (CHM) is an autonomous body working covenantally and cooperatively with associations, conferences and the covenanted ministries of the UCC to promote its work among Hispanics in the United States, Puerto Rico, and Latin America.

The Council for Racial and Ethnic Ministries (COREM) was established as a recognized body of the UCC in 1983. COREM is composed of two representatives each from PAAM, CAIM, CHM, UBC, and MRSEJ. This body meets twice a year to plan a common agenda. It collaborates with appropriate program and mission bodies of the UCC so that resources for racial and ethnic ministries will be effective and relevant. It also advocates for racial and ethnic concerns within the UCC.

THE RELATIONSHIPS AND FUNCTIONS

Local Churches

The basic unit of the United Church of Christ, a local church is composed of persons who are organized for Christian worship and for the ongoing work of Christian witness. All persons who are members of a local church of the United Church of Christ are thereby members of the United Church of Christ.

Associations

Situated within a conference, an association consists of all local churches in a geographical area, all ordained ministers holding standing therein, all commissioned ministers of that association, and those licensed ministers granted vote. Associations determine the standing of local churches in the United Church of Christ and grant, transfer, and terminate ordained ministerial standing in the United Church of Christ.

Conferences

A conference consists of all local churches in a geographical area and all ordained ministers, commissioned ministers, or licensed ministers holding standing or vote in its associations (or in the conference itself when acting as an association). These, as well as delegates selected by local churches of the conference, may vote when the conference meets. The standing of a conference as a body of the United Church of Christ is determined by the General Synod.

General Synod

The General Synod, the representative body of the United Church of Christ, consists of delegates chosen by the conferences, voting members of boards of directors of covenanted ministries, and ex-officio delegates. It carries on the work of the United Church of Christ; provides for the financial support of this work; calls and elects officers of the denomination; nominates and elects members of boards of directors of covenanted ministries; nominates and elects most Executive Council members; establishes and maintains the United Church of Christ's national headquarters; receives and disburses funds contributed for the support of the United Church of Christ and its covenanted ministries; and determines ecumenical and interchurch relationships.

The Executive Council, which acts for the General Synod ad interim, consists of members named by the Synod plus representatives of covenanted ministries and other United Church of Christ bodies and groups. It coordinates and evaluates the work of the United Church of Christ; is responsible for policies related to the church's mission in its national setting, including the health of the covenanted ministries in relationship with one another and their accountability to the Synod; supports the church's spiritual and financial wealth; performs corporate functions of the Office of General Ministries; facilitates the Synod's business; and is a focal point for planning and budgeting.

OF THE UNITED CHURCH OF CHRIST

Covenanted Ministries

There are four covenanted ministries of the United Church of Christ, each carrying out its work in covenantal relationship with the General Synod and Executive Council and in interactive partnership with local churches, associations, conferences, and national bodies of the church. Each nominates and elects its executive minister, who participates in the Collegium of Officers. Each has its own budget, charter and bylaws. Each participates in the Mission Planning Council.

Justice and Witness Ministries enables and encourages all settings of the church to engage in God's mission globally by direct action for the integrity of creation, justice, and peace. It encourages and assists the church in speaking prophetically on matters of justice, power, and public policy and confronting racism, ageism, classism, and other expressions of injustice and alienation. It supports the ministry of service on behalf of the poor, forgotten, oppressed, and those marginalized by stigma and discrimination based on sexual orientation or disability. It may witness on behalf of Synod policies.

Local Church Ministries encourages and supports local churches in the fulfillment of God's mission. It encourages them to shape their life and mission in partnership with one another and with other expressions of the church. It promotes the vocation of all members and the leadership of laity and clergy and facilitates a system of placement. It nurtures stewards and coordinates and promotes churchwide mission funding. It strives for the vitality of local churches as inclusive, accessible communities of mission, evangelism, church development, education, unity, worship, nurture, and justice.

The Office of General Ministries cares for the spiritual life, unity, and well-being of the church; nurtures its covenantal life and its ecumenical and interfaith relationships; and facilitates the visioning, planning, coordination, and implementation of the total mission of the church.

Wider Church Ministries encourages and supports the United Church of Christ as part of the global church and encourages support of United Church of Christ ministries around the world and the nation. It strengthens relationships with partner churches. It oversees participation in the Common Global Ministries Board, a joint venture with the Christian Church (Disciples of Christ), and, through it, the sending and receiving of missionaries. It supports institutional ministries in health care, education, disaster relief, and social services; coordinates volunteer ministries; and promotes interfaith dialogue, global education, and advocacy.

Associated and Affiliated Ministries

The Pension Boards — United Church of Christ, an affiliated ministry of the United Church of Christ, provides employee benefit and ministerial welfare programs.

United Church Foundation, Inc., an associated ministry of the Executive Council, offers a broad range of United Church of Christ investment opportunities to strengthen mission.

The United Church of Christ Joins with Others

The preamble to the constitution, voted in 1961 and honored to this day, states that the Purpose of the United Church of Christ is "to express more fully the oneness in Christ of the churches composing it, to make more effective their common witness in Him, and to serve His kingdom in the world." To fulfill this mandate the UCC cooperates with others in the National and World Council of Churches and in various specialized ecumenical groups.

Through the National Council of Churches, UCC people work with those from other denominations in preparing accurate translations of the Bible, addressing hunger issues, supporting farm workers, using the mass media to tell about Christianity and providing joint approaches to overseas mission. The council also develops approaches to education, addresses the concerns of women in ministry, offers support to minority education programs, and prepares missionary education resources (through the Friendship Press).

The United Church of Christ is actively involved in the diverse work of the World Council of Churches, Churches Uniting in Christ (formerly known as the Consultation on Church Union), the World Alliance of Reformed Churches and the Formula of Agreement that in 1998 brought our denomination into full communion with the Reformed Church in America, the Presbyterian Church, USA, and the Evangelical Lutheran Church in America.

Financing the Work of Our Denomination

The money for this work comes from the many congregations and members scattered throughout the nation. The United Church of Christ General Synod formulates the program of the church and adopts a unified budget as a goal for church giving. Each local church shares in this mission through its offering.

Our Churches Wider Mission (OCWM) is the name given to the special mission budget that enables the conferences and covenanted ministries to perform their mission and ministry. Where does the money go? Monies contributed by local churches go to the treasurer of the conference of which the church is a member, and a portion is set aside to support the conference program. The treasurer in turn sends an agreed-upon percentage of the remaining amount to the Office of General Ministries that apportions the money according to the budget and payment schedule adopted by the Executive Council.

About the Work of Our Church

Fill in the spaces in the following sentences. The answers to some of these are given in this chapter, but on others you will have to do some research. Your minister can suggest resources where the answers may be found.

1. The name of the governing body of the denomination is _____
    _____

2. The governing body of my denomination meets every _____ years.

3. In between these meetings, the business of the denomination is carried on by a body called the _____.

4. The number of members in my denomination is approximately _____
    By including children in the estimate of our large Christian community, this figure would he increased by approximately 500,000 people.

5. The general minister and president of the United Church of Christ is
    _____.

6. The name of our church newspaper is _____.

7. The total program adopted by the General Synod and carried out by the United Church of Christ is called _____
    _____

8. The number of local churches in my denomination is _____.

9. These local churches are organized into _____ conferences.

10. Name two under-represented groups or constituencies in the United Church in Christ. _____
    _____

11. Some of the special projects carried out as part of our church's mission to America include the following (see the list in the Resource Section):

    _____

    _____

    _____

    _____

21

The Church As Teacher

From the very beginning the Christian church has considered teaching as an important part of its ministry, just as Jesus considered it an important part of his ministry. The Gospel of Matthew ends with the well-known command, "Go therefore and make disciples, . . . baptizing them, . . . teaching them to observe all that I have commanded you." Christians are disciples, which means "learners," but they must also be teachers. The Christian church in its broadest sense is where Christian learning takes place and where Christian teaching occurs. It is within the Christian community that people of all ages are nurtured in the Christian faith and mission. It is within the Christian community that they are able to feel the love of God and can respond to God in loving trust. It is within the church that they are nurtured in loving and outgoing concern for others. In other words, it is in the Christian community that people learn to love God above all else and to love others as themselves.

Much learning takes place as Christians meet with other Christians in the home and while involved in the work and worship of the congregation. It also takes place as they participate in its specially planned program of Christian education.

How the Church Has Organized for Christian Education

Throughout its history the Christian church has felt the need for special classes and schools to fulfill its teaching ministry in the best way possible.

During the early centuries there were catechetical classes that trained people for membership in the church. There were also higher schools for leaders; the most famous was at Alexandria in Egypt.

During the Middle Ages there were schools connected with monasteries and cathedrals. The church did most of the teaching that was done during that period in history.

During the Protestant Reformation catechisms were written and widely used in teaching. The Lutheran and Reformed churches have made much of catechetical teaching ever since.

Time and again colleges and universities have come from the church. For example, in our own country, Harvard, Yale, and Princeton were all started chiefly to train ministers. Our United Church of Christ has seven seminaries for that purpose as well as an historic relationship with eight others.

In our country's pioneer days it was not unusual for a congregation to have its own school (called a parochial school) with its own teacher and a schoolhouse alongside the church.

In 1780 Robert Raikes started the first Sunday school in London. He gathered together a few children and paid a woman to teach them. Sunday schools spread rapidly throughout the churches of England and America.

Vacation church schools began in New York City about 1900. Children were idle in the streets of the city. Teachers were idle. Buildings were idle. All came together to start vacation church schools.

Weekday church schools were started in 1914 in Gary, Indiana, where the public school superintendent agreed with the pastors to free the children a short while each week for religious teaching.

This is not the whole story by any means, but it shows that the church has been a teacher from the very beginning. Sometimes, when there were no other schools, the church taught everything—reading, writing, and arithmetic as well as religion. Now, because there are public schools for all children in our country, the church can focus on teaching the Christian faith and the Christian way of life. This is a big enough task. It includes much more than teaching facts about the Bible and the church. It includes everything that helps children, youths, and adults to grow in the Christian life.

The Teaching Work of Our Denomination

Our United Church of Christ has accepted Jesus' commission to go into all the world and teach his disciples to do all that he commanded. Local Church Ministries carries a primary responsibility for this teaching vocation. Through its Worship and Education Ministry, and its Publications, Resources and

Distribution Ministry, it produces holistic approach to the United Church of Christ's mission in education. It seeks to develop an educational program and adequate resources based on:

1. an understanding of how the church is empowered to educate people for Christian life and higher education; and
2. life span approaches in education that are informed but not limited to knowledge about the human life cycle or by cultural and environmental factors affecting human learning.

Local Church Ministries lifts up a vision of education in the UCC in which everyone is engaged in learning throughout life in a variety of settings and issues. That vision requires the reclaiming and reforming of the church's educational mission, the minister's historic office as teacher, and the committed partnership of the laity and clergy in the teaching ministries of the church. The educational work of Local Church Ministries is based on the following:

1. The mission of the church begins with God, who creates, sustains, and redeems the whole world and life.
2. People of all ages and conditions are nurtured by continual inquiry into Christian faith and experience as well as by the general search for wisdom, justice and beauty in human society.
3. The foundations for the UCC's educational mission are found in
   a. the biblical record of God's covenant with Israel and of the apostolic witness to Jesus Christ;
   b. the nature, purpose, and faith of the church;
   c. the informing presence of the Holy Spirit;
   d. the history and traditions of the UCC;
   e. the Christian understanding of human beings and society; and
   f. the social and cultural spectrum of the world in which we live.
4. In each new age the church must struggle for educational models and methods that respond to the current needs and lead to change.
5. God teaches us through unexpected sources. Christians therefore must be continually open to all seekers and servers of truth.
6. Education in the UCC is informed and strengthened by the racial, ethnic, cultural, and geographic diversity of its members. That diversity reflects the world in which we live.
7. Education in the UCC must be rooted in biblical and historic Christian faith, in the call to be disciples of Christ in the world, and in the fresh and transforming revelation of God in our time.

How Important Is the Teaching Ministry of the Church?

A discussion of the following situations may help us to determine how important the teaching ministry is to the church.

1. A minister decided to do away with the church's Sunday school. Instead, on Sunday morning there was to be a church service for all the people aged twelve and over. Meanwhile, there would be something like a Sunday school in another part of the building for those under twelve. There would also be the usual organizations for young people, men, and women, but they would not meet on Sunday morning. What do you think of this plan? What might it gain? What might it lose? What would you lose if your church school were closed? Would the attendance at the church service increase or decrease? If all people attended church service faithfully each Sunday, would that be enough?

2. Suppose a certain church had five hundred dollars to spend either on paying the fees for church school teachers to attend summer conferences or on a stained-glass window. Which would be the better way to spend the money? Why?

3. Suppose a church were to give up all its teaching work—Sunday church school, vacation church school, weekday church school, confirmation class, and everything else. What would happen to it in fifty years? Why?
   What would happen to its children and young people? Would most of them become faithful church members? Would their lives be as fulfilling or as useful as they would have been if the teaching had been kept up? Why?

4. Some church schools have separate classrooms for each class, much like public schools. Some have a library of books to which teachers and students can go for more information on the Bible, the life of Jesus, Christian beliefs, and the like. Some have a Sunday session lasting more than an hour. Some have a committee on Christian education, which lays plans much as a school board does for the public schools. Some even pay their teachers. Do such things make for a more effective teaching ministry?

5. If you were inviting a friend of your own age to join your church youth program, what reasons would you give?

Write here your conclusion about the importance of the teaching ministry of the church.

Your Congregation as a Teacher

List here all the places you can think of where teaching is being done in your church. Include any in which other things besides study are part of the program. To answer some of the questions that follow, members of the class must do some research and conduct some interviews.

When we speak of the whole church engaged in teaching, what do we mean?

In what ways are *you* teaching others?

How many people does it take to carry on the formal teaching work of your church? (In your answer, include all officers, teachers, leaders, and committee members who do some form of teaching.) _____
Is this a large or a small number? Is there any other agency in your community where as many people give as much time without pay?

Who supervises your church school? _____

If your church employs a director or minister of Christian education, write his or her name here. _____

The Church As Teacher

What is the percentage of attendance in your Sunday church school? (Divide the average attendance by the total enrollment.) _____
Is the percentage high or low?

How many hours a week do you spend at church learning to be a Christian?

_____

How many hours a week do you spend on "homework" in connection with your studies? _____
Is this amount adequate to be really helpful to you?

_____

About how much money does your church spend on its teaching work each year? (Your pastor, director of Christian education, or church treasurer can give you an approximate figure.) _____ Is this sufficient to carry on an effective educational program?_____

How effective is the teaching work of your church? Are people of all ages learning how to become better Christians by studying together and reflecting together on the Christian way of life? Interview a number of teachers to find out what they think needs to be done to improve the teaching work of your church. What can you do to help? Write on this page as many ways as you can think of whereby you can help to make the teaching work of your church more effective. (They may be very simple things that you can do.)

22

The Church As Friend

Jesus himself was a friend to all who needed him in any way. Much of his ministry was spent in bringing health and new life to those who were sick in body and spirit. We have it from his own lips that this was his great purpose in life. One sabbath day in the synagogue at Nazareth, Jesus read from the book of Isaiah. There are many passages that he might have read, but this is the one he chose:

> The Spirit of the Lord is upon me,
>   because he has anointed me to bring good news to the poor.
> He has sent me to proclaim release to the captives
>   and recovering of sight to the blind,
>   to let the oppressed go free,
>   to proclaim the year of the Lord's favor.
>   —Luke 4:18-19

In the early church, care was given to the poor and needy. For example, in Acts 6:1–6 we read that seven men were elected to take charge of the daily distribution of food; in Acts 11:29–30 we find Paul helping to take a sum of money for the relief of the church at Jerusalem in a time of famine. This was the spirit of Jesus at work in the world.

Wherever Christianity went, people who had been mistreated—women, children, slaves—were dealt with more thoughtfully. This was the spirit of Jesus at work.

During the Middle Ages there were organizations of monks who gave themselves to the care of the sick. Some of these monks made lepers their special concern.

The Church Concerns Itself with Befriending People

In our own day we find many instances of the church befriending people directly. Health care is one area in which this befriending takes place. Compassionate health care means being responsive to the needs—and the problems—of those being served. In India, as in the United States, health care in rural areas is often difficult to find. Wider Church Ministries is a partner with the Comprehensive Rural Health project in India. It trains health care workers who live in rural villages. They learn how to take care of their neighbors and friends. Those who are trained then train others who in turn teach others the basics of health care.

For the native Americans of the Big Mountain Indian Reservation in northern Arizona, life has become difficult because the government is attempting to move them off their land. Many of the young people have moved away; water is scarce; electricity has been cut off; the elderly are left without resources. When the students of the UCC-related Westminster College (in Salt Lake City, Utah) heard of their plight from a fellow student, they immediately began to collect food, money, and clothing to send to the reservation. Their sensitivity to the concerns of native Americans stems in part from the activities of the Native American Student Group and the campus-wide Indian programs that received a grant from the Local Church Ministries.

In Zimbabwe, Christian Care works with the more than 700,000 people who have fled the violence in Mozambique. It provides safe shelter and medicine, runs schools and refugee camps, and helps organize cooperatives. Christian Care is the development arm of the Zimbabwe Christian Council. It receives funds from both the Church World Service and Witness programs and Wider Church Ministries of the UCC.

The purpose of the United Church of Christ Fellowship of Reconciliation (FOR) is the resolution of human conflict in light of God's love for all the world. To that end, the FOR rejects violence as an option for solving problems. Along with the Disciples Peace Fellowship, with which it has met, it seeks to avoid bitterness and contention in dealing with controversy; promotes good will among races, nations, and classes; and identifies with those who are victims of injustice and exploitation.

The indigenous people of Latin America are among those with whom the two fellowship groups identify. These people are often at the bottom of the economic and social ladder, exploited and abandoned by social services. In

Ecuador, the UCC Common Ministry to Latin America and the Caribbean as well as the Disciples Peace Fellowship provide grants to the Brethren United Foundation. The foundation's staff works with the Indians and the rural poor near Quito, giving them legal aid, general education, and classes in agricultural development. Slowly, but steadily, the foundation's insistence on justice for the poor is sowing the seeds of reconciliation.

Native Americans living in Tennessee became refugees when ordered out of their homeland by President Andrew Jackson. Many current reservations essentially continue this legacy. To highlight their concerns, the UCC-related Rocky Mountain College in Billings, Montana, joined with seven tribal colleges to sponsor a Native American Needs Awareness Program. The program, supported by a grant from the Council of Higher Education and Local Church Ministries brought together native Americans active in their churches and trained members of the Montana-Northern Wyoming Conference to help them interpret native American concerns.

The Church Is Concerned About Solving Social Problems

Some social problems are on a community level, some are on a national level, and some are of a global nature. Sometimes it is a local church or a city federation of churches that is concerned. Sometimes it is the entire denomination, the National Council of Churches, or the World Council of Churches. The UCC is working on all these levels to solve social problems in the following areas.

1. *Troubled youths.* The UCC-related Hoyleton Youth and Family Service programs in Hoyleton, Illinois, provide a broad range of services to today's young people. They include a runaway hotline, a Youth-at-Risk program, counseling for families, and a special Teen Pregnancy Prevention program. When youths cannot be kept in their homes, Haven House provides emergency shelter and counseling to help the young people. Eventually, the youths either return home or move to a residential treatment program, such as the Hoyleton Children's Home.

2. *Homelessness.* At first glance, Westchester County appears to be an affluent New York suburb. But the First Congregational Church of Chappaqua found that homelessness is a reality for some forty-five hundred in Westchester, the majority of whom are children. In fact, they found that the average age of a Westchester homeless person is six. They also found that the

normal practice of housing a homeless family in a motel was needlessly expensive and demoralizing for a family.

With that in mind, they developed the Adopt-a-Family project. Its purpose is to find housing for the homeless and help them become self-sufficient members of society.

The church adopted a homeless family consisting of a mother and four small children, and it stood by her as she sought housing, fought the bureaucratic red tape that so often stood in her way, secured furniture, and searched for a job. In addition to helping the family, the church wrote an extensive report that it gave to the county with the hope that "the information will move someone in County government to address a terrible situation." The report also serves as a guide for other churches contemplating adopting a homeless family.

3. Justice for the Poor. According to the Valley Interfaith Project of Phoenix, Arizona ranks second lowest in the nation in high school graduates per one thousand of population. It has the highest child death rate in the nation, an air quality that ranks forty-fifth of fifty states, and nearly half a million residents with no health insurance. The project, which receives grant funds from Local Church Ministries, works with Arizona's poor to effect change. Working with people of different ethnic, religious, and cultural backgrounds, translators are present at its meetings to share the concerns of Spanish- and English-speaking citizens.

4. AIDS. In 1989, the former United Church Board for Homeland Ministries began organizing the AIDS National Interfaith Network (ANIN). The network, now based in Washington, D.C., provides technical expertise for those in the religious community involved with AIDS ministries. It is a major AIDS lobbying voice in Washington. Both ANIN and Wider Church Ministries, where HIV/AIDS concerns are now lodged, recognize that it is often the religious community that offers the first—and sometimes the only—care and comfort for people with HIV/AIDS.

The UCC/Disciples Common Ministry in Latin America and the Caribbean is also responding to the needs of people with AIDS. Booklets written in Portuguese have been distributed throughout Brazil and have been sent to Angola and Mozambique, where Portuguese is also spoken. A booklet entitled SIDA y Pobreza, or AIDS and Poverty, has been published by the Christian Church (Disciples of Christ) in Argentina.

5. *Home and family relations.* The church is seeking in every way it can to make home and family relations more Christian, for it is on the home that

community improvements depend. It is for this reason that our Worship and Education Ministry of Local Church Ministries studies questions of family life and provides churches with materials.

6. *Racial justice.* The General Synod strongly opposes racial prejudice and segregation. Justice and Witness Ministries has the responsibility to educate United Church of Christ members on the Christian attitude toward racial justice and to consult with local churches in meeting this problem.

7. *Citizenship and political life.* The General Synod believes that many of the decisions affecting the good of the nation depend on informed citizens using the channels of government wisely. To help our people know about important laws before the Congress, Justice and Witness Ministries has a Washington office.

Your Congregation as a Friend

You may have to go to the officers of the various organizations in your church for the answers to the following questions, or else your pastor can help you.

How does your congregation show Christian friendliness?

_____

_____

Did your church make a contribution last year to any of our denomination's hospitals, homes for children, or homes for the elderly? If so, how much?

_____ Were there any gifts other than money?

What? _____

What does your church do by way of helping needy families within its own membership? _____

_____

How does it cooperate with community welfare agencies and institutions or organizations such as the United Way? _____

_____

The Church As Friend

What is done by your church or any part of it in the way of visiting the sick?

_____

_____

Do you have members who keep in touch with the ill and the elderly? If so, what do they do?_____

What does your church do for prisoners? For children who need adequate recreational facilities? For unemployed people? For people in trouble?

_____

_____

_____

What does your church do to extend friendship to people of other churches? of other races? of other nationalities? What does it do for newcomers and strangers in the community?

_____

_____

_____

What does your church do about drug and alcohol abuse, pornography, gambling, lotteries, and so on? What does your church support that contributes to people's well-being?

_____

_____

_____

What other ways can you discover in which your congregation acts as a friend?

_____

_____

_____

Your Denomination as a Friend

The class might borrow someone's file copies of the United Church News for a year or two back and see what the United Church of Christ has done to befriend other people around the world. For instance, has Wider Church Ministries sent money and/or food to victims of droughts, earthquakes, tsunamis, floods, or hurricanes? Has Local Church Ministries supported the work of racial and ethnic minorities? What special efforts to combat racial injustice are presently being sponsored by Justice and Witness Ministries?

What Can You Do?

You will surely want to take your part in the Christian friendliness that has been a part of the church's life from the beginning. Perhaps you will want to start now, as a class. Here are some suggestions:

1.   Work out a plan for visiting regularly every shut-in person within the congregation, perhaps taking along a copy of the church bulletin or a recording of the minister's sermon.

2.   Make your own offerings to support Our Church's Wider Mission.

3.   Take part in any offerings for one of our hospitals; one of our homes for children, the elderly, or the mentally retarded; or for a family of refugees.

4.   Organize a joint meeting of youths of your own age but different from you in racial and ethnic heritage.

5.   Plan a party for younger children of the congregation.

6.   Help with a Christmas collection of toys (new and used) for poor children or a Halloween collection of money for the United Nations Children's Fund.

7.   Provide games and play equipment for children who have none.

8.   Make a contribution to one of the special projects currently authorized for the support of the United Church of Christ.

23

The Church As Missionary

Have you ever tried to find the words missions or missionary in the Bible? They just aren't there! Yet, many Christians believe that missions are the most important thing in which the church is involved.

The Bible's word for missionary is *apostle,* one of the great New Testament words. *Apostle* is the Greek way of saying "one who is sent" (the literal meaning of the Greek word in the New Testament). Missionary is a Latin word that means the same thing, and we have taken the word over into English.

Jesus was a missionary, and he told the disciples: "Go . . . and make disciples of all nations, baptizing them in the name of the Father and of the Son and of the Holy Spirit, teaching them to observe all that I have commanded you" (Matthew 28:19–20). One of the greatest of Jesus' followers was Paul, who began his most important book with the introduction "Paul, a servant of Jesus Christ, called to be an apostle [missionary]" (Romans 1:1). From the earliest New Testament times, various missionaries helped new churches and converts express the Christian faith. Missionaries have been and are today both men and women, both lay people and clergy. They may be ministers, teachers, librarians, doctors, nurses, community organizers, agricultural or development workers, administrators, or businesspeople. Today, missionaries are selected in response to the needs of our partner churches overseas.

Many other men and women came after Paul. Most of them are unknown to us. The names of some are famous in history as the founders of great churches and sometimes as the patron saints of whole nations, such as Patrick, missionary to the Irish; Augustine, missionary to the English; Ansgar, missionary to the Norse people; Robert Morrison, missionary to the Chinese; David Livingstone, missionary to the Africans; Frank Laubach, missionary to the world's illiterates; Ida Scudder, missionary to India; and Mother Teresa, missionary to the world's poor. Today missionaries from churches all around the world serve in other countries to tell of God's love for all people and to work with God's people everywhere. Some also come to the United States to share and work with us.

Our Church as World Missionary

From the earliest days of our church, mission work has been part of its life; John Eliot began his mission to the Indians of New England in the 1630s. In fact, the first book printed in America was Eliot's translation of the Bible into the Algonquin Indian language. Ever since Eliot's time Native American Indian people have shared in the life of our church and shared its mission. In the early 1800s a famous Supreme Court case, Worcester v. Georgia, pitted a missionary against the state on behalf of Native American Indian self-determination.

The American Board of Commissioners for Foreign Missions had its beginnings in a haystack. In 1806 several Williams College students in Massachusetts sought refuge from a rainstorm in a haystack. Their prayer meeting in that setting led to the determination to start an overseas mission. (For more on this meeting, see page 117.) They began a movement that led to the founding of the first American foreign mission society in 1810. In its early years the board of this society represented several denominations, but later it came to be Congregational in sponsorship. Today the work of that board and of the Evangelical and Reformed church continues through Wider Church Ministries.

Here are a few landmark dates and events in the history of our denomination's worldwide adventure in missions:

1812—First American missionaries sail for India.

1819—First missionaries sail for the Sandwich Islands (Hawaii) and also to the lands of the Bible, the Middle East.

1830—First American missionaries begin work in China.

1833—First missionaries to Indonesia.

1835—Missionaries go to work with Zulu people in South Africa.

1852—Missionaries begin work in Micronesia jointly with Hawaiian churches.

1869—Missionaries go to Japan.

1872—Missionaries go to Mexico.

1873—Missionaries go to Spain and Austria.

1880—Missionaries go to West Central Africa (Angola).

1893—Missionaries go to East Central Africa (Mozambique and Zimbabwe).

1902—Philippines mission is established.

1921—Our missionaries begin work in Honduras, answering the call to "come over and help us."

1923—African congregational churches establish Galangue Mission in Angola.

1943—Our church launches a program of world service to meet the needs of refugees and war victims after World War II.

1946—Our denomination, as part of the United Andean Indian Mission, begins rural work high in the Andes in Ecuador and also begins work in Ghana at the invitation of the African churches there.

1960—A missionary family is sent to Taiwan to teach in a Christian university sponsored by many cooperating churches.

1965—Missionaries go to Zambia to work after expulsion from Zimbabwe, formerly Rhodesia, where Africans are struggling for independence from colonial rule.

1973—Missionary families begin to help educate ministers in Costa Rica and Botswana.

1979—Missionaries go to Nepal.

By action of General Synod:

1981—The Evangelical Church of the Union (EKU) in the former East and West Germany, now called the Union of Evangelical Churches (UEK) in Germany, established "church fellowship."

1983 — The Presbyterian Church in the Republic of Korea (PROK) and the United Church of Christ establish mission partnership.

1985—The Pentecostal Church of Chile and the United Church of Christ affirm mission partnership.

1987—The United Church of Christ in the Philippines (UCCP) and the UCC/USA reaffirm mission partnership.

1989—The United Church of Christ reaffirms Middle East Council of Churches as primary mission partner in the Middle East.

1991—The Evangelical Presbyterian Church of Ghana and the UCC/USA reaffirm mission partnership.

1993—The United Church of Jamaica and the Cayman Islands and the UCC/USA affirm mission partnership.

1999—The Protestant Church of East Timor and the UCC/USA affirms partnership.

The United Congregational Church of Southern Africa and the UCC/USA affirm partnership.

The Congregational Church in American Samoa and the UCC/USA affirm mission and ministry partnership.

2003—The Union of Evangelical Churches in Germany (UEK) and the UCC/USA affirm Kirchengeminschaft.

The Church of South India and the UCC/USA affirms a full communion relationship.

Ask your minister for a copy of the *Annual Report* of the United Church of Christ, the newsletter *In Mission,* and the *Calendar of Prayer,* all of which link us with people and churches in mission throughout the world.

Our Church as Missionary in the Homeland

The Pilgrims and Puritans came to early New England with a vision of a holy commonwealth. They believed that Christians were called by God to develop public institutions to serve the people. For a long time only church members were eligible to vote in Massachusetts and Connecticut. Church buildings were called meeting houses and were used during the week for the town meeting (the political governing structure) and on Sunday for worship.

It was natural that people of these traditions and experience should worry about new settlements and towns on the frontier. Would they have Christian influences? Would they have enlightened governments? The answers to these questions were not left to chance. Missionary societies were formed to be sure that clergy would be available to organize churches and that there would be experienced people to start schools, run the government, and build community institutions. Whenever pioneers ventured into new communities, the church went with them. To our ancestors in the faith, the frontier was both a challenge and an opportunity.

People from the German Reformed and Evangelical synod traditions were involved in migrations from one section of the country to another. Their Bibles, catechisms, and hymnbooks were in their saddlebags or wagons as they moved to new places. They took with them, too, their concern for a vital church presence, for education, and for such instruments of mercy as hospitals and homes for the elderly and the deprived.

The United Church of Christ has benefited in a special way from various patterns of immigration. The Pilgrims, of course, were the first immigrants to take their place in our faith story. People of German background formed the backbone of the Reformed and the Evangelical parts of our story. But the list of immigrant peoples who formed churches that are part of our tradition and life is very long—Africans, Armenians, Hungarians, Chinese, Filipinos, Japanese, Koreans, Mexicans, Puerto Ricans, Samoans and other Pacific Islanders, and Scandinavians—to mention only a few. The United Church of Christ is richer because of this diversity. The homeland mission today naturally includes a ministry of presence with new immigrant groups.

The mission to America is one of church extension—extending the church to new places. Often this means helping a new group of people to form a church, gain strength, and become self-supporting. Sometimes church extension means reaching new constituencies that have not previously been a part of the United Church of Christ. Through Our Church's Wider Mission monies the whole church helps this to happen.

The labor movement began for a reason. Workers, whether they be coal miners, assembly line operators, or teachers, were being exploited. Low wages meant higher profit. Dignity, and often safety, became secondary considerations. The intrinsic worth of each individual proclaimed by the church was at odds with corporate practice.

After many years of struggle, labor unions established a balance of power with employers. In the 1980s, however, collective bargaining and unions came under attack. Striking workers were simply replaced by others hungry for jobs. The legal right to strike became an occasion for punishment.

To help restore the rights of working people, the former United Church Board for Homeland Ministries convened the Religious Committee for Work Place Fairness. Justice and Witness Ministries continues this partnership. The interfaith board of the Religious Committee for Work Place Fairness calls on churches to "proclaim the moral basis for the rights of working people."

Just as the church proclaims that each person must be mindful of others, the Religious Committee for Work Place Fairness proclaims that the commitment to community is essential.

The TECHE Area Ministry in New Iberia, Louisiana, is a cooperative venture of four local churches, the South Central Conference, and Local Church Ministries. These small, predominantly African American congregations share joint programs in education, evangelism, community outreach, and stewardship under the leadership of a pastor. Part of the pastor's duties is to identify and train several lay leaders in biblical studies, theology, and pastoral skills to help serve the four churches as licensed ministers. The conference and Local Church Ministries give both financial assistance and leadership consultation to their cooperative programs. It is anticipated that what is learned from this ministry will be helpful to other small churches with similar needs.

Project ElderNet of the Beatitudes Center for Developing Older Adult Resources (Center DOAR) in 1992 held a conference, FOCUS on Older Adult Ministries. Funded in part by a grant from the former United Church Board for Homeland Ministries, Project ElderNet brings together leaders from seven denominations concerned about developing meaningful ministries with aging people and their families. One result of the project will be the publication of a manual describing ways that other communities can develop collaborative ministries on behalf of the most rapidly growing part of our population, the elderly.

In 1979, the Congregational Church of Algonquin, Illinois, had two hundred members. Today, it has over fourteen hundred members. When it needed to expand its facilities to keep up with its growth, a loan of $450,000 from the Church Building Revolving Loan Fund, now lodged in Local Church Ministries was an integral part of its $1.2 million expansion. The church is an active supporter of a homeless program, a food pantry, Habitat for Humanity, and a variety of programs to help those with substance abuse problems. The church also has ten choirs and considers music a critical and important part of its ministry.

Between 1964–1988, Trinity United Church of Christ in Chicago, an historic African American congregation, received loans and grants to support its growth and the building of a new church. In 1989, it received the largest loan ever given to a local church "to erect a house of worship" in the amount of $2,250,000 from the Church Building Revolving Loan Fund. Later transferred to the United Church of Christ Cornerstone Fund, this loan was paid in full ahead of schedule. In combination with secular loans, the church completed and dedicated its new house of worship, with a seating capacity of 2,700 in 1994 and added administrative and program space in 1996.

Trinity Church, during these years, also founded Trinity Community Housing Corporation (for senior housing), Trinity Acres Corporation (to operate a senior housing project), Trinity Day Care Corporation (for child care) and Trinity Conservation Corporation (a landscaping business and flower shop). It has grown from a congregation of several hundred members in 1964 to become the largest church in the United Church of Christ, with three services each Sunday and more than 12,000 members.

Child Watch is a program of the Children's Defense Fund that replaces statistics with the faces of children. The idea of Child Watch is to teach people about the needs of children, to show them what reality is like for many children, and then to share ways to make a difference. Through its affiliation with the Child and Family Working Group of the National Council of Churches of Christ, Local Church Ministries cooperates with six other organizations, including Kiwanis, the Junior League, and the American Association of Retired Persons (AARP), to gain a deeper understanding of the ways that social policy affects children.

Child Watch brings volunteers to Washington for three days of training. They then return home and assemble teams that visit hospitals, shelters, and schools. The teams learn about the state of children—and then discuss ways to address the problems they find.

As these various programs show, the homeland mission agenda is diverse. At its most basic, it involves an attempt to change national priorities as expressed in federal and state budgets so that more attention is given to the needs of people — jobs, education, health care, community development, and equal opportunity. It is expressed in community organizations dealing with bread-and-butter issues, such as the location of nuclear plants, the rampages of urban renewal, the destruction of key elements of the neighborhood, or access to adequate health care and housing. The mission is also expressed through a Christian ministry in national parks and other leisure-related efforts. It involves both church enablement and shaping community structures to achieve more humane values.

Finally, the homeland mission is expressed in the ways in which your local church acts to meet the needs of the hungry, the hurt, the homeless, the disenfranchised, and the victims of crime.

Your Congregation as Missionary

Once more look at your own home church—this time to discover all the ways in which it is doing missionary work. Then answer the following questions.

How much did your congregation give for missions last year?
$ _____ (The treasurer of your congregation or your pastor can tell you.) Can you picture this money making its way to various places in America and beyond to tell the story of Jesus?

Some of the acts of friendliness about which we spoke in chapter 22 can be counted here also. Showing friendliness to neighbors in the next block is mission work as truly as showing friendliness to people oversees. A hospital or a children's home in America is a mission just as truly as a hospital or a home in Asia. Has your congregation supported a missionary? If so, write the missionary's name here. _____

Does your church have a partnership with an overseas church? If so, write the church's name and country here. _____

How many places can you find where your congregation is teaching about the church's mission? In the church school? In youth groups? In women's groups? In men's groups? In vacation church schools? Do you have special services or festivals each year on world and homeland missions?

Does your church help to support some special missionary work? If so, write the projects here.

_____

_____

_____

What does your church do to reach people in your community who belong to no church at all?

_____

_____

What Can You Do?

1. Be a missionary in your neighborhood. Help people who need help. Bring people who belong to no church to your church. Tell your pastor about such people so she or he can visit them.

2. Prepare a missionary play and give it in church school, at a youth group meeting, or elsewhere.

3. Plan a program of movies, slides or videos showing the missionary work of our church in its various fields.

4. Visit a nearby new church or mission.

5. Think seriously about the possibility of becoming a missionary someday, either at home or abroad. Encourage your church or conference to host a missionary from abroad.

PART SIX
Some Questions to Face

24

My Decision — What Will It Be?

Time and again when Jesus was living here on earth he said, "Follow me." He said this to Simon Peter, Andrew, Matthew, and others. He did not want followers for his own sake. No, he wanted people to follow him for the new life it would bring to them, for the good they could do to others, and for the sake of the realm of God so that it might grow among people.

There is an interesting story in Matthew 19:16–22 that tells how Jesus called a certain young man to follow him. Read it now in your Bible and answer the following questions in your own words.

What questions did the young man ask Jesus? _____

_____

What was Jesus' answer? _____

_____

Why wasn't the young man satisfied with this answer? _____

_____

What more did Jesus say that he could do? _____

_____

Why would Jesus make such a demand? _____

_____

Was it because the poor need help? _____

Was it because money meant too much to this young man? _____

Was it for both reasons? _____

Draw a picture that would illustrate this story.

Jesus Calls You to Follow Him

You cannot see Jesus with your eyes or hear him with your ears as did the rich young ruler, but Jesus is calling you to become his follower too. His call reaches you in many ways. Throughout the sessions of this confirmation class his call has been coming to you. Whenever you read Jesus' words or hear them read from the Bible, he is speaking to you. Every hymn about him brings his call to you. Every sermon that presents Jesus and his message is a call to you. Every picture of him on canvas or on paper or in a stained-glass window presents a call to you. Every church school lesson about him brings a call to you. Through every faithful home he calls you to follow him. Through every Christian person he calls to you.

You Must Decide What Your Answer Will Be

A decision has to be made sometime for or against Jesus. The rich young ruler either had to follow Jesus, or else he had to turn away. He could not do both. He had to decide one way or the other. The same is true for you. You cannot possibly live both following Jesus and not following him. It must be one or the other. You cannot possibly care for what he cared for most—God and people—and at the same time live for money or popularity or a good time. It cannot be done, just as a person cannot walk east and west at the same time. Hear what Jesus said in the Sermon on the Mount: "No one can serve two masters; for either he [or she] will hate the one and love the other, or he [or she] will be devoted to the one and despise the other" (Matthew 6:24).

You are the only one who can make this decision. Your parents or guardians, your teachers, your pastor, and your friends can help you; but when all is said and done you must decide for yourself which way your life is to go.

Do You Have Some Bothersome Questions?

Sometimes questions arise in a young person's mind as she or he thinks about confirmation. Let's look at several of these briefly.

Must I have some definite "experience" before I have a right to be confirmed? Should you hear Jesus' call in some special way? Must there be some moment when you are altogether sure in some mysterious way that you have taken Jesus as your Lord and Savior? The answer is such an experience is not necessary. Some people have an experience of this sort, and others do not. Paul had a startling experience (see Acts 22:6–11) on the road to Damascus, and he could look back during the rest of his life to the very moment when he became a Christian. As far as we know, Timothy never had such an experience. He was reared in a good home, and he grew quietly and naturally into the Christian life (2 Timothy 1:5; 3:14–15).

Do I have to be sure about everything before I can be confirmed? Again, the answer is—you do not have to be sure about everything, but you ought to be sure about a few things. You ought to be sure of the following:

1. There is a God whose child you are and who loves you more than any human being can.
2. Jesus Christ is God's Child and your Savior and Lord, to whom you must give your full loyalty and love.
3. God is willing to help you in your daily living through the guidance of the Holy Spirit.
4. You really want to be a member of the church of Jesus Christ and help in its witness to the realm of God on earth.

If you are sure enough of these beliefs to "bet your life" on them, then a good many other matters can wait to be cleared up later.

You do not have to understand everything in the Bible, for it is doubtful if there is anyone who understands everything in it. You do not have to understand fully how the world could be made out of nothing, how God can hear so many people praying at the same time, or exactly what life will be like in the hereafter, for there are real differences of opinion among sincere Christians on some of these points. Be sure of as much as you can, and beyond that be willing to put your trust in whatever seems reasonable and in keeping with God's goodness.

Do I have to be entirely good before I can be confirmed? The answer again is no. Otherwise the church would have no members. We who are in the church are not perfect. We are striving to become more and more like Jesus, but we must say with Paul, "Not that I . . . am already perfect; but I press on . . . toward the goal for the prize of the upward call of God in Christ Jesus" (Philippians 3:12–14). You are not asked to be perfect. You are asked to be sorry (to repent) for what you have done wrong (your sins), ask God's forgiveness, and intend with all your heart to live the Christian life. You are asked to put Jesus Christ and his way, God and God's will, above everything else in your thoughts and your actions. You are asked to do what Paul asked of Timothy in 2 Timothy 2:15; 2:22; and 3:14–15.

After you are confirmed, you will fall short of your best intentions many times, and it will be necessary for you to repent and to ask God's forgiveness over and over again. But you will keep on trying to grow in every way possible into the fullness of Christ's example. (See Ephesians 4:13–15.) With God's help you will succeed more and more as the years go by.

savage

25
Why Do I Need The Church?

The best way to think about this question is to imagine yourself in a community without a single Christian church. People have come from all over to work there. At first there are not any permanent homes for the families. You live in a trailer. There are housing developments, shopping centers, and schools, but there is no church or church school. How would you feel?

Would you feel like the writer of Psalms 42 and 43? (Originally these were one poem.) The writer was evidently a Jew who lived in rather wild country far to the north, where the river Jordan was only a stream and where the people did not share his faith in God and made fun of him because of his beliefs. One day, while sitting by the stream listening to it tumble noisily over the rocks, his thoughts went back to the services of the Temple in Jerusalem, and as he remembered them he became homesick for them, as Psalm 42:4 clearly shows:

> *These things I remember,*
> > *as I pour out my soul:*
> *how I went with the throng,*
> > *and led them in procession to the house of God,*
> *with glad shouts and songs of thanksgiving,*
> > *a multitude keeping festival.*

It is not always easy to keep in close touch with the church all your life, even when there are churches in your community. Sometimes Sunday brings other activities that seem more attractive than attending the church services. Some of your friends may not care for the church, and they may taunt you as did the psalmist's companions, saying "Why do you go to church? You can get along without it."

It may be that you are now going to church because your parents or guardians urge you to do so. But the day will come when you are on your own. Then you must know for yourself whether you need the church so much that you cannot get along without it. When you are confirmed you are saying publicly that you do need the church and that you will use its services to grow into the best sort of Christian you can.

How Does the Church Help a Person?

There are people all around you who have belonged to the church for many years—your parents or guardians, your church school teacher, friends of the family. Ask some of these people what the church has meant to them, how it has helped them. List here the answers you get.

You have been in the church for only a short time, even though you may have been baptized as a baby and may have grown up in the congregation, but you have been in it long enough to experience some of the ways in which it helps people. Think about these ways.

Now imagine that you are urging a friend of yours, or some neighbor, to join the church. Suppose that person asks you why he or she should join or what you get out of belonging. What would you say? Write here what you would answer.

Why You Need the Church

Below are six reasons why you may need the church. Examine each one carefully. Is it true for you?

1. *You need the church because it can help you to live up to the best you know.* Every now and then someone says he or she can live just as well without the church as with it. Such a person stands a poor chance of constantly living up to his or her best. Once a week or more often we need to be with people who stand for what is good and who help us to stand for it too. We need to be reminded regularly through hymns, prayers, preaching, sacraments, and teaching that there is a God who is good and wants us to be good. Otherwise we might forget it. If we were to get away from the church, we might be able to keep on living our best for six weeks or even six months; in six years, however, we would almost certainly have slipped backward. Most of us are simply not strong enough to be our best without the help of other Christians. Don't think that this cannot happen to you. It is amazing how many young people make a wreck of their lives.

To Think About. Do a little imagining again. Your family has moved to a strange community. The church of which you are a member is far away, and you have not joined one of the churches in your new community. Week after week passes, and you do not go inside a church. The friends you make are not church people and do not look at things as church people do. How long would you keep thinking of Christ and his way of life? For six weeks? six months? six years? You would be an exceptional person, indeed, if you could continue to pray regularly each day and seek God's help for your daily living, and if you could keep high Christian standards for long. The church is there to help you live up to the high standards of living laid down by Jesus Christ.

2. *You need the church to help you deepen your understanding of what is best.* It is not enough to live up to the best you now know. You must also year by year get a deeper understanding of what is best because your present way of thinking may be only partially right.

Anne grew up in a community where "foreigners" were thought to be somewhat beneath her own people. She has since changed her mind about this. She has talked with foreigners, eaten with them, worked with them, prayed with them, played with them. She has come to a deeper understanding of the parenthood of God and the human community and the kind of life she should live. It was the church that gave her this understanding.

The church can give you more help in deepening your understanding than any other institution can. It alone will go with you all through life to the very end. In a few years you will leave school. In all probability you will also leave your present home. School and home help for a short while, but the church will keep with you to the end.

The church is the only place where Jesus' personality is held before your eyes week in and week out. In him you can see God's will most clearly. With his help you can correct your wrong notions and set your life straight. Through accepting his teachings you can deepen your understanding of the highest and best in life. (See 2 Peter 3:18.)

To Think About. How sure are you that your present way of looking at various matters is right? What about your attitude toward people who are different from you? toward money? a good time? What about your purpose in life? Would there be anything lost if you had to go through life thinking about each of these matters exactly as you do now? Suppose you were to get away from the church; could something else take its place in deepening your understanding of what is best? Could the public schools? the books you read? the movies? newspapers? TV? anything else?

3. *You need the church to help you in times of sin, disappointment, and sorrow.* You may not have had too many bad experiences as yet, but unfortunately you will at some time. You will do things that you would give everything you possess to undo. You will hang your head in shame and wonder if anybody living is as bad as you are. You will be disappointed again and again. You will want something badly and not get it. You may hunt long for a job without finding one. The plans you lay will not all work out, and the things you hope for will not all come true. Sorrow, too, is bound to come sooner or later. There is always the possibility of illness or accident, and there is the certainty of death someday—for you and for those you love.

When sin, disappointment, or sorrow comes into your life, where can you turn? In the church you can hear the comforting assurance of the grace of God, promised in the gospel to all that repent and believe: "Have I any pleasure in the death of the wicked, says the Lord God, and not rather that they should turn from their ways and live?" (Ezekiel 18:23). In that assurance you can turn your back on your sins and try again, trusting in God's forgiving love.

In the church you can hear the old, old words that have helped so many in times of trouble:

> *The Lord is my shepherd, I shall not want;…*
> *Even though I walk through the darkest valley,*
> *I fear no evil;*
> *for you are with me.*
> *—Psalm 23:1,4*

There, too, you will hear the words of Jesus in the Sermon on the Mount, "Blessed are those who mourn, for they will be comforted" (Matthew 5:4). There you can find the minister and the friends who will stand by you and help you in every sort of difficulty. (See 1 Corinthians 12:26a.)

To Think About. If all the churches should disappear from your community, where would you turn in times of trouble? Have you ever gone to your pastor for help in any difficulty? Would you do so if the need arose? How would you go about consulting your pastor?

4.   *You need the church in times of joy and accomplishment.* The second part of 1 Corinthians 12:26 points this up. Christians are always happy to help other Christians celebrate. When young people fall in love and are married in the church, all the members like to come and be happy with the couple. When a new baby comes into a home, the church rejoices and welcomes the baby into the community of the church. When people join the church, the members are there to shake the hands of the new ones in Christian community. When members graduate from high school or college or win special honors of any sort, the church rejoices with them. Christians need this community of joy as much as they need the community of sorrow.

5.   *You need the church because it gives you the chance to find yourself in service.* A young woman came to her minister and asked if there were any needy families in the community whom she could help in her spare time. Was that a strange request? Why should a person go out of her or his way to be of service to others? Because a Christian needs to think far more about helping

others than of getting anything for herself or himself. We cannot be fully happy nor can we truly love God unless we do for others at least as much as we do for ourselves (see Luke 10:25–28). We have not fully found ourselves unless we have given of ourselves to others.

The church offers you some of your best opportunities to find yourself in service. Here, before many years are past, you can teach a church school class and have the deep satisfaction of guiding children or older people into the Christian life. Here you can serve on the consistory, church council, or one of the church's organizations, thus helping in all the good work that is being done. Here you can place on the offering plate money that will fly through the air—as it were—to preach the gospel, to heal the sick, feed the hungry, help the suffering, and teach others both in our own country and abroad.

To Think About. Why is it that we are truly happy only when we forget ourselves in service to others or to some good cause?

6. *You need the church to help you to a life that is forever rich and full.* As Christians, we believe that God has made us to live forever. This is a great thought, almost too great for our small minds. The good and happy life on which the church starts us during these years here on earth will continue forever! How we need the church!

To Think About. Imagine yourself ten thousand years from now looking back on your days on earth. How would you feel when you realized that by getting away from the church and what it stands for you had missed the full life for ten thousand years? Read Jesus' story of the rich man and Lazarus in Luke 16:19–25. This story has a message for us.

Can you think of other reasons why you need the church? Write them down. Which one of these reasons seems most important to you? Which one would you stress in urging a friend to join the Christian community?

26
Why Does The Church Need Me?

One of the most beautiful ways of thinking of the church is that it is a body with many parts, or members, but one spirit running through it all. The individual Christians are the different parts, and the spirit running through it is the spirit of Christ. There is one whole chapter in the Bible that speaks of the church in this way, 1 Corinthians 12. Read this chapter.

The Church Needs the Help of All

Now begin to think of your home church as being like a body. A body has many members—foot, hand, eye, ear, and so on. In the same way your church has many members—fifty, one hundred, five hundred, or even a thousand. In a body, not all the members have the same work, but each carries out its own task. The foot is for walking, the hand for grasping, the eye for seeing, the ear for hearing. So in your church not all the members have the same work. The church school teacher teaches, the choir member sings, the organist plays, the officers manage the affairs of the church. Many others carry their faith into the home, workplace, and community.

In a body each member needs all the other members. The eye needs the foot; the foot needs the hand; and so on. In a church each member needs all the other members. The church school teacher needs the choir singer; the choir singer needs the elder or deacon; and so on. In a body all the members are important, and all their work is necessary. So in a church the work of all its members is important and needed.

The church needs you to help do its work. When you are confirmed you affirm your membership in a body whose spirit is the spirit of Christ.

You must do your part as a member, whatever that part is. If you do your job well, you help the body to function as it should; if you fail, the whole body will suffer. The next section explains five ways in which you can help the church. Consider them carefully.

How Can You Help?

1.   *You can help the church with your time.* There are many jobs that require somebody's time, as you probably discovered if you interviewed church leaders as suggested on page 133. Look for jobs you can do. Consult your pastor, the custodian, the consistory, your parents or guardians, and others. List the jobs you discover and set a time for getting them done.

Turn to pages 203–204 and study "My Involvement as a Member." If you are not sure what some of the statements mean, ask your pastor to explain them.

2.   *You can help the church with your talents.* You may have some outstanding talent, such as the ability to sing well, to play some instrument, or to speak forcefully to a group. But many other talents that are less conspicuous are needed too. You may have a talent for cooking, for fixing broken furniture, for cleaning up after others, or for any one of a large number of tasks that the church needs done from time to time.

3.   *You can help the church with your money.* You may not have much money, but that need not keep you from giving what you can. Some people feel that we should follow the Old Testament rule (see Leviticus 27:30) of giving a tithe (one-tenth) of our income to the church and other good causes. Others like to follow Paul's suggestion in his first letter to the Corinthians (16:2) of giving each week according to what one has received. This is called proportionate giving, since it is in proportion to what one has received. What is important is to have a system and to stick to it.

The church needs to know how much it can count on. It is for this reason that most churches focus on stewardship one Sunday each year, when all members are called on to indicate how much they feel they can give during the coming year. Some churches set up two funds, one for the local church and one for benevolence (doing good to others). Many churches provide their members with a package of envelopes in which they can make the contributions they have agreed to make each Sunday. After you are confirmed you may be receiving a set of these. The church needs such regular giving.

Why Does the Church Need Me?

The important question for you now is what you can give. This is a question for you to face with your own conscience, but it may help to discuss in class what might be done. Someone might volunteer the information that he or she receives a weekly allowance of five dollars and that he or she earns ten dollars more each week delivering magazines. How much should this person give? Should he or she give a tenth, that is, one dollar and fifty cents a week? Would it make a difference in the amount he or she should give if his or her family were fairly well off or were poor? In what way? Would it make any difference if the church were struggling to make ends meet or if it had no financial worries?

4. *You can help the church with your attendance.* The story is told of a church in a European village that is lighted only by the candles that members bring with them from their homes. When the time for the service arrives, each member takes a single candle and goes to the church. There the members take their seats in their regular places and put their lighted candles on the stands in the pew. If the members are all present, the church is well lighted and there are no dark spots. But if a member is absent, her or his place is dark.

The story is worth thinking about. Does a church member go to church only for her or his own sake? Does it make any difference to the other members whether she or he comes or not? Does it make any difference to the minister? Do you think it makes any difference to God? Does all of this apply only to the church service, or is it true also for church school, the youth groups, and the like? Is coming half the time half as good as coming regularly? Why, or why not?

What services or meetings within the church should you attend each week?

5. *You can help the church with your life style.* There is nothing that aids the church more than good living on the part of its members, and there is nothing that hurts it more than bad living on the part of even one of its members. People outside the church are almost sure to say: "Look at that person. That's a church member, and yet see how that person lives." They conclude that the church amounts to very little. One evil life can hurt the church as much as ten good lives can help it. This seems unfair, but things often work out this way.

Is it worse for a church member to be dishonest, selfish, prejudiced, lazy, or a poor parent than it is for someone outside the church to be that way? Why, or why not?

You Must Be a Good Steward

The church speaks to us a great deal about stewardship. It tells us that every-thing we have is not our own but that it really belongs to God. We are merely caretakers, or stewards. The church gets this idea from Jesus. One day he told a story that states clearly what he thought about this matter. Read the parable of the talents in Matthew 25:14–30.

The man who went away into a far country stands for God. The servants stand for all of us. The talents (pieces of money) represent everything we have—our money, our time, our abilities. And so the point of the story becomes clear. Everything we have is really not ours. It comes from God, and it is really God's. We are to use it not for ourselves but for the doing of God's will. All our money—not merely the part we give to the church—is to be used in the way that will best advance God's realm. The same is true of all our time, all our abilities, and our very lives.

This is what the church means by stewardship, and it calls you to be a good steward of all that God has entrusted to you. The church needs good stewards if God's realm is to flourish on earth.

What Will You Do?

The question then comes to you personally: What will you do in and for your church? You must answer now, and you will have to face the question anew each day throughout your life. The church needs you at all stages of your development, for there is more work to be done than there are hands to do it.

Now that you have been thinking about why and how the church needs you, perhaps you would like to draw up your own statement on "My Duties as a Church Member." Write in the space below (or on a separate sheet of paper if you need more space) what you believe to be the duties you will assume when you are confirmed.

Some churches make a special effort to enlist all their members in some activity by getting each member to sign a checklist such as the one that follows and to place it on the offering plate on a certain Sunday, thus making an offering of his or her services to God and the church.

Go over this list of activities and think prayerfully about the work in the church that you might be able to do after you are confirmed. Not all items will interest you now, nor would you be able to do all at your age or with your abilities. Check the ones you think you can do. Then talk to your pastor about the possibility of doing some of them.

My Involvement as a Member

Desirous that my membership in our church will be helpful to the church and meaningful for me and that through the church my influence may count in some clear way for the realm of God, and having thought over the uses I make of my time, I here set down my purpose and belief that out of the week's 168 hours I should give at least _____ hours to the activities of my church.

The items in the life and work of our church that I have checked below are those in which I have special interest or for which I have special talent. As my time and ability permit, I will take part in the activities mentioned.

If the task is one in which you are now active, mark it with an A. If it is one in which you are interested and willing to take part, mark it with an X.

Worship

_____ Daily private worship

_____ Sunday church services

_____ Midweek services during Lent

_____ Preparatory services

Any other? _____

Christian Education

_____ Sunday church school

_____ Youth organization

_____ Women's organization

_____ Men's organization

_____ Boy Scouts

_____ Girl Scouts

_____ Dramatics

Any other? _____

Active Leadership

_____ Teach in the church school

_____ Sing in the choir

_____ Serve on the consistory or church council

_____ Help with the annual Stewardship Sunday

_____ Assist on the committee for social gatherings of the congregation

_____ Serve as Boy or Girl Scout leader

_____ Play the piano

Any other? _____

Family Life

_____ Daily private worship

_____ Sunday church services

_____ Midweek services during Lent

_____ Preparatory services

Any other? _____

Christian Fellowship

_____ Visit occasionally, on the pastor's request, people who are not members or are inactive

_____ Help with games and other play activities at parties, picnics, and so on

_____ Entertain a small group of members at my home occasionally, perhaps at the pastor's suggestion

_____ Visit sick or shut-in members

Any other? _____

Social Action

_____ Help to provide play space and equipment for children of the community who do not have these things

_____ Try to make the business life of our community more Christian

_____ Try to understand other races and religious groups and work with them in matters of interest to us all

_____ Help to root out drug and alcohol abuse, immoral magazines and videos, and so on

_____ Work for world peace

Any other? _____

Evangelism

_____ Be on the lookout for people who do not go to any church, and invite them to attend church and church school with me

27
What Does Confirmation Mean?

The day of confirmation has been a truly great day in the lives of many people in many lands through many ages. Many years ago around the Mediterranean Sea men and women, young and old, received the blessing of confirmation with "prayer and the laying on of hands." On the Sunday you are confirmed, or on Sundays near that day, thousands around the world will join you in making confirmation vows and in kneeling for the same blessing with "prayer and the laying on of hands."

What Confirmation Will Mean to You

In the introduction to this book there was a brief account of how confirmation began in the early church. An explanation was also given of what the word *confirm* means. Look again at pages 1 and 2 and refresh your memory of what was said there. What is it that is made firmer and stronger when you are confirmed?

The twentieth-century edition of the Heidelberg Catechism also offers an explanation of catechism, one that emphasizes God's role in the service. It explains that "while you thus confirm your baptismal vows, God on [God's] part, through this laying on of the hands of [the] minister, claims and accepts you as [God's] own, renews [the] covenant with you, and assures you of present and future needful grace. Confirmation, the laying on of hands, is God's act of love to you."

Many of the chapters in *My Confirmation* have tried to give you a better understanding of what confirmation means, but now we want to sum up briefly what has been said.

When your name is called by your pastor and you go forward to receive the blessing of confirmation, that step should mean primarily two things to you:

1. That you are making a public announcement of your decision to follow Jesus Christ, and

2. That you are assuming full responsibility as a member of the church.

You never may have said publicly that you intend to follow Jesus Christ. Now you will be going on record before God, your family, your friends, and the members of the congregation that you mean to follow Christ, that you are answering his call to you with an audible yes, that you mean henceforth, as far as you are able, to trust in God, to care for others, to care for yourself, and to seek the realm of God.

In different words, you will be saying what Patrick, the great missionary to Ireland, said back in the fifth century:

> *Christ be with me, Christ within me,*
> *Christ behind me, Christ before me,*
> *Christ beside me, Christ to win me,*
> *Christ to comfort and restore me,*
> *Christ beneath me, Christ above me,*
> *Christ in quiet, Christ in danger,*
> *Christ in hearts of all that love me,*
> *Christ in mouth of friend and stranger.*

When you go forward, you will not as yet have said publicly that you intend to follow Jesus. When you come back to your seat, you will have said it.

Depending on the rules of your own congregation, as a full-fledged member of the church you can vote in a congregational meeting, help elect the officers of the church, and yourself be elected to an office, including that of elder or deacon. There are other duties too that we have already addressed in an earlier chapter. You will be expected to help the church with your time, your money, your attendance, and your life. In short, you are growing up in the eyes of the church. You are no longer to be regarded as a child, but as an adult.

Your Confirmation Will Mean Much to Others Also

There are others to whom your confirmation will mean a great deal. No greater joy can come to Christian parents who brought their children to the church in baptism than to see these children accept for themselves the responsibilities of full church membership. Church school teachers, too, take real satisfaction in the confirmation of those whom they have taught. For most ministers the high point of the year is the moment when they lay their hands in blessing on the heads of those whom they have come to know and love through many hours of study together. The members of the congregation generally see their numbers and strength growing with these new members, and they look back with solemn memory to the day when they themselves were confirmed.

God, we believe, rejoices at the sight of people being confirmed, and God's Spirit goes forth to them in many ways to bless them and guide them and strengthen them.

Your confirmation will mean even more to you if you will remember all that it means to others.

After Confirmation

The twentieth-century edition of the Heidelberg Catechism gives the following advice to those who have just been confirmed:

> You are now confirmed. Never forget what you have done. Often recall the lessons, hymns and prayers, your confession, vows and kneeling, the laying on of hands, the solemn blessing. Now that you are a full member of the church, stand firm. Be faithful to your vows. Beware of backsliding—the quiet, slow, gradual slipping away from daily faithfulness in private and in public Christian duty. Be careful to cultivate a tender conscience and a devotional spirit. Receive the Lord's Supper regularly. Always come to the holy communion humbly, sincerely, trustfully. At every communion, recall your confirmation vows, and carefully look over your past life to see how they have been kept. Cultivate great love for the church. Take a deep interest in all [its] work. Regularly go

to the house of God and heartily join in worship. Be active in church work. Faithfully use your gifts for the salvation of others. Study the Bible. Read it daily and prayerfully. Use all the best helps you can. One great help is the sermon. Listen carefully to it. Lead a life worthy of the calling to which you have been called.

We need to remind ourselves constantly what being a confirmed member of the church means, and the farther away from our day of confirmation we get the more we need such reminders.

It is easy enough to make fine promises. It is not always so easy to keep them. Simon Peter found that out to his sorrow. One day he said to Jesus, "I will lay down my life for you" (John 13:37). Those were brave words, but not many hours later Peter swore that he did not even know Jesus (Mark 14:71).

The vows that you take at your confirmation—will you keep them the following Sunday, throughout the year, and so long as your life lasts? Will you be a loyal member of the church and a faithful Christian all your days?

May God help you ever to remain true to your confirmation vows!

The Order for Confirmation

If you are to enter fully into the service of confirmation, it is important that you understand the service itself. Ask your minister for a copy of the order he or she intends to follow. The following is an outline of The Order for Confirmation from the *Book of Worship* and comments. If the order your church follows is different, these study suggestions will still help you to understand the service.

1. *Opening Sentences*
    These words are taken from the Bible.

2. *Questions of the Candidates.*
Write out the meaning of each one.

_____

_____

_____

3. *Affirmation of Faith*

Bear in mind how old this is and how many people have used it to profess their faith when they joined the church.

4. *Prayer of the Candidates*

Before reading the suggested prayer, write here what you yourself would want to ask of God in the moment before kneeling to be confirmed. _____

_____

_____

_____

5. *Act of Confirmation*

Any one of several blessings can be said. Your pastor will tell you which one he or she intends to use.

6. *Prayer of Confirmation*

7. *Question About Participation*

8. *Welcome into the Christian Community*

9. *Greeting of Christian Love*

10. *Prayer*

11. *Benediction*

Review Questions on Part 6

1. Why do you want to join the church of Christ?

2. What has the church already done for you?

3. What can the church do for you?

4. What can you do for the church?

5. What does Jesus and his church require of you?

6. How much time should you give to the church?

7. How much money should you give?

8. What is meant by *stewardship*?

9. What are your duties as a member of the church?

10. What does the word *confirm* mean?

11. What is meant by the *laying on of hands?*

12. What does confirmation mean to you?

My Creed

Write what you now believe about the following:

God

Jesus Christ

The Holy Ghost

The Bible

The Church

Myself

Sin

RESOURCE SECTION

The Contents of the Bible in Brief

Genesis. Very old stories of the creation of the world and the beginnings of the Hebrew people down through the life of Joseph. (The name of the book means "beginning.")

Exodus. The story continued through the flight of the Hebrews from Egypt and their first wanderings in the desert. (The name means "a way out.")

Leviticus. Chiefly a collection of laws about the right way to conduct the worship of that day.

Numbers. Takes up the story of the Hebrew people once more, covering most of the forty years of wandering in the desert. The book gets its name from the censuses recorded in it.

Deuteronomy. Principally laws—some about the right way to worship and some about the right way to live. (The name means "second law.")

Joshua. The story of the Hebrew people entering the land of Canaan under Joshua's leadership.

Judges. These judges did not sit in courtrooms. A better word would be rulers or leaders.

Ruth. A beautiful love story that pleads for racial tolerance.

1 and 2 Samuel, 1 and 2 Kings. Four books (originally only two) by a common author (or authors), making one continuous history. They cover five hundred years from before the first king of Israel until after the last one. Samuel, Saul, David, Solomon, Elijah, and Elisha are among the great characters of this history.

1 and 2 Chronicles, Ezra, Nehemiah. Four more books of history edited by one person. They go over the same ground and more but were written several centuries later than Samuel and Kings, and this time by a priest, or at least someone who thought as a priest thinks.

Esther. A thrilling story of a Jewish girl who was a beautiful queen and a brave patriot.

Job. A great drama on a difficult question: Why do good people suffer?

Psalms. A hymnal containing a hundred and fifty hymns, gathered together from several collections by the Jews over many centuries and still used for worship today.

Proverbs. Another collection—but this time of wise, pointed sayings.

Ecclesiastes. The word means "preacher." This preacher is discouraged with life, as his words plainly show.

Song of Solomon (or Song of Songs). Ancient love songs used at weddings. They have also been taken to represent the love between God and God's people.

Isaiah. Chapters 1–39 contain the words of a young nobleman who was a prophet (one who speaks for God) in a time of great danger. Chapters 40–55, written in exile two hundred years later in Babylon, are a message of faith and hope. Chapters 56–66 were written after the return from exile to correct religious tensions between the Jews who had been in exile and those who had remained in Jerusalem.

Jeremiah. Another great prophetic book, whose main point is that religion is a personal matter between God and each of us.

Lamentations. Five poems lamenting the capture of Jerusalem by its enemies.

Ezekiel. A priest in exile looks forward to a new and better day for his people.

Daniel. Stories about Daniel, plus four strange yet hopeful visions that he had.

Hosea. A prophetic book whose message is God's forgiving love for us.

Joel. A prophetic message in a spell of locusts and dry weather.

Amos. A strong prophetic message that God wants right living above all else.

Obadiah. A prophetic message for the nearby Edomites at a time of trouble.

Jonah. A prophetic message that God loves people of all nations—really a foreign missionary sermon.

Micah. A prophetic message much like that of Amos.

Nahum. A message of joy that the great enemy, Assyria, seems about to fall.

Habakkuk. A prophetic message on another difficult question: Why do evil people seem to get along so well?

Zephaniah. A prophetic message about the terrible Scythian invaders; pointing out that they are carrying out God's judgment.

Haggai and Zechariah. Two short books with the same purpose—to encourage people to rebuild the Temple that had been destroyed by Nebuchadnezzar.

Malachi. A message of warning to get ready for God's judgment. (The name of the book is Hebrew for "my messenger.")

Matthew. A life of Jesus, stressing his teachings.

Mark. A second life of Jesus, stressing his actions.

Luke. A third life of Jesus, written by a doctor, stressing Jesus' healing ministry.

John. A fourth life of Jesus, written to make him known to people who were used to Greek ways of thinking.

Acts. The history of the early church and the story of Paul.

Romans. A letter by Paul, explaining his idea of the main Christian message.

1 Corinthians. A letter by Paul, answering various questions that the Christians of Corinth had asked him.

2 Corinthians. A letter by Paul (or several put together), defending himself and his work against attack.

Galatians. A letter by Paul, opposing the idea that everyone who wanted to become a Christian must first go through the ceremony of becoming a Jew.

Ephesians. A letter, possibly written by Paul, stressing the importance of the church.

Philippians. A letter by Paul—of thanks and Christian encouragement.

Colossians. A letter by Paul, warning against the notion that the way to be good is by punishing our bodies.

1 Thessalonians. Paul's first letter and the oldest book in the New Testament. He is glad the church at Thessalonica is coming along well. He offers advice.

2 Thessalonians. A second letter to the same church, clearing up a mistaken idea and urging church members not to be lazy or disorderly.

1 Timothy, 2 Timothy, and Titus. Three letters on how to be a church leader and how to do church work.

Philemon. A brief letter by Paul to the owner of a runaway slave.

Hebrews. A long letter showing why the writer believes that the Christian faith is clearly better than the Jewish faith.

James. A practical letter on how to live the Christian life day by day.

1 Peter. A letter to Christians who face persecution.

2 Peter. A letter of encouragement urging Christians not to give up hope that Jesus will return.

1 John. A splendid letter on Christian love.

2 John. A brief letter to a "lady and her children."

3 John. A brief letter to a church member named Gaius.

Jude. A brief warning against false teachers who might hurt the church.

Revelation. A glorious vision, written for the encouragement of Christians facing persecution and put in a way that the Roman officials would not
understand. It is really a coded message.

The Church Year

Christians have their own year. It is the same length as the calendar year, but
it begins and ends around December 1. It too has seasons, but they are not
winter, spring, summer, and fall. They are Advent, Christmas, Epiphany, Lent,
Easter, Ascension, Pentecost (Whitsunday), and Trinity. The church year is
divided into two parts of about six months each. The first is called the half
year of our Lord because it retraces from start to finish the earthly life of Jesus.
The second is called the half year of the church because it begins with
Pentecost, the anniversary of the church's beginning, and deals with the life of
the church and the life of Christians today. Most churches follow the church
year to some extent. Here is a brief outline of it.

The Half Year Of Our Lord
(from about December 1 to about June 1)

Advent—The four Sundays before Christmas. Advent means "the coming." In
it we prepare our hearts to celebrate Jesus' coming into the world,
receive him into our own lives and live in expectation of his return at the
end of history.

Christmas—Christmas Day and one or two Sundays following. In it we rejoice
over our Lord's birth.

Epiphany—January 6 and from one to six Sundays following (depending on
when Easter falls). Epiphany means "showing forth." We remember at
this time the "showing forth" of our Lord to those who were not Jews,
the Magi who came to see him from afar.

Pre-Lent Sundays—The three Sundays before Ash Wednesday. They have Latin
names that you sometimes see on church calendars: Septuagesima,
Sexagesima, and Quinquagesima, meaning seventieth, sixtieth, and fiftieth. These Sundays are the ones nearest to the seventieth, sixtieth, and
fiftieth days before Easter. They are a bridge between the brightness of

the Epiphany season and the more sober tones of Lent.

Lent—The forty-day period (not counting Sundays) from Ash Wednesday to Easter. Lent is forty days long in remembrance of the forty days Jesus spent in the wilderness being tempted. During Lent we remember the life of Jesus and his death on the cross. We also look into our own hearts and lives to see if we are worthy followers of his. Lent closes with Holy Week, which begins with Palm Sunday and includes Maundy Thursday and Good Friday.

Easter—Easter Sunday and the five following Sundays. This is the most joyous time of the church year. In it we rejoice that our Lord is alive forevermore and that we too will live eternally. (Easter Day falls on the first Sunday following the first full moon after the spring equinox—March 21. This means that Easter may fall on any date from March 22 to April 25.)

Ascension—The Thursday that comes forty days after Easter, and the following Sunday. This is the close of the half year of our Lord because it marks the completion of his life and work on earth.

The Half Year Of The Church
(from about June 1 to about December 1)

Pentecost, or Whitsunday—The seventh Sunday after Easter. It is the anniversary of the birth of the Christian church. (Pentecost means "fiftieth" and is the fiftieth day after Easter. The term Whitsunday goes back to the time when those who were about to be baptized wore white robes.)

Trinity—The eighth Sunday after Easter. On Trinity Sunday we think of God as being three in one—Father, Son, and Holy Spirit, or Creator, Redeemer, and Sustainer.

Sundays after Pentecost—On the Sundays that follow we think of the present-day life of the church and of Christians. Such special days as Church School Day, Labor Day Sunday, Christian Education Sunday, World Communion Sunday, Reformation Day, All Saints Day, and Thanksgiving Day fall in this period.

The Span of Jesus' Life

6 B.C.	His Birth
Historians made a mistake of 6 years when they redated everything from his birth.	Boyhood
6 A.D.	Visit to the Temple (Age 12)
	Working in the carpenter shop and thinking about the work of God
27 A.D.	Baptism (Age 33)
	Only two years of ministry. The Gospels dwell on these years— especially the last week.
29 A.D.	Crucifixion (Age 35)

The Meanings of the Symbols on Page 220

    1. *Hand of God.* The three fingers extended refer to the grace of our Lord, the love of God, and the communion of the Holy Spirit.

    2. *Alpha and Omega.* The first and last letters of the Greek alphabet, symbolizing that Jesus Christ is the beginning and end of all things. (See Revelation 1:8.)

    3. *I H S.* The first three letters of the Greek word for Jesus.

    4. *Lamb of God* with the Banner of Victory. Symbolizes the risen and triumphant Christ. The three-rayed nimbus around the head signifies divinity. The white pennant, representing Christ's body, is attached to a cruciform staff, thereby signifying his death on the cross. If the lamb were lying down, that would change the symbolism to suffering rather than triumph.

    5. *Quatrefoil.* The outer parts of four interwoven circles, representing the four Gospels or their writers.

    6. *Descending Dove.* Symbolizes the Holy Spirit.

    7. *I N R I.* A symbol for Jesus. The letters are the initial letters for the Latin inscription placed on the cross: **Iesus Nazarenus Rex Iudaeorum** (Jesus of Nazareth, King of the Jews). (See John 19:19.)

    8. *Calvary, or Graded, Cross.* The empty cross symbolizes the risen Christ, the Redeemer of humankind. The three steps in descending order represent faith, hope, and love. (See 1 Corinthians 13:13.)

    9. *Celtic, or Irish, Cross.* The circle, representing eternity, with the cross symbolizes the eternal quality of Christ's redemption.

    10. *Fleur-de-lis.* Conventionalized form of the lily, flower of the Virgin Mary, symbolizing the annunciation. It is used also to represent the Trinity.

    11. *The Two Tablets.* Represent the Ten Commandments.

    12. *Sheaf of Wheat, and Bunch of Grapes.* Often used on communion tables to represent the bread and wine.

    For the meaning of other symbols that are used in your church, see *Our Christian Symbols* by Friedrich Rest (United Church Press) or some other book on symbolism that you can get from your library.

1. _____ 2. _____ 3. _____

4. _____ 5. _____ 6. _____

7. _____ 8. _____ 9. _____

10. _____ 11. _____ 12. _____

Bible Verses to Know

1. *Commit These to Memory*

Exodus 20:2–17	The Ten Commandments
Psalm 23	The Shepherd Psalm
Psalm 100	Psalm of Praise
Micah 6:8	God's Requirements
Matthew 5:3–10	The Beatitudes
Matthew 22:37–39	The Two Great Commandments
Matthew 28:19–20	Jesus' Last Command
John 3:16	God's Great Love

2. *Become Familiar with These*

Genesis 1	The Creation Story
Genesis 11:31–7:2	The Story of Abraham, Isaac, and Jacob
Exodus and Deuteronomy 29-31,34	The Story of Moses
Ruth	The Story of Ruth
1 Samuel 16-1 Kings 2:12	The Story of David
Isaiah 6:1–8	The Call of Isaiah
Isaiah 53	God's Suffering Servant
Matthew 5-7	The Sermon on the Mount
Matthew 25:14–30	The Parable of the Talents
Matthew 25:31–46	The Parable of the Last Judgment
Mark 16:1-8	The Story of the Resurrection of Jesus
Luke 2:1–20	The Story of the Birth of Jesus
Luke 10:30-36	The Parable of the Good Samaritan
Luke 15:11–32	The Parable of the Forgiving Father
John 4:19–24	What True Worship Is
John 10:11–18	Jesus the Good Shepherd
John 13:34–35	Jesus' New Commandment
John 17	Jesus' Prayer for His Followers
Acts 2	The Story of Pentecost

Acts 22:6–11	The Conversion of Paul
Romans 1:16	The Power of the Gospel
1 Corinthians 11:23–25	The Institution of the Lord's Supper
1 Corinthians 13	The Love Chapter
Ephesians 4:1-16; 4:22-5:2	Growing Up in Christ
Philippians 2:1–11	Imitating Christ's Humility
Hebrews 11	The Faith Chapter
Revelation 21:1–7	A New Heaven and a New Earth

Hymns Suitable for the Confirmation Service

The following hymns are suitable for use in the confirmation service. The class may select the one that seems to say best what its members want to say in the service.

"Jesus, I Live to Thee" was written by a minister of the former Reformed church in the United States, Henry Harbaugh. In your Bible turn to Romans 14:8 and Philippians 1:21. Do you think that Dr. Harbaugh had thoughts like these when he wrote this hymn?

"O Jesus I Have Promised" was written by John E. Bode on the occasion of the confirmation of his daughter and two sons. When should this be sung in the service—before or after the rite of confirmation?

"We Would Be Building" is another hymn that was written for young people. It is by a minister of our church, Purd E. Deitz. What sort of building does this hymn speak of?

"My God Accept My Heart This Day" and "Now in the Days of Youth" and "I Was There to Hear Your Borning Cry" are also great confirmation hymns.

In a Church Member's Vocabulary

A

Adoration. Paying honor to God; intense regard and love.

Adultery. Unfaithfulness to the marriage vow.

Advent. The season of the church year that consists of the four Sundays before Christmas.

Almighty. Having power over all; all-powerful.

Alms. An offering given for charity or for relief of the poor.

Altar. A place of sacrifice. In the Old Testament it was a raised structure on which an animal or incense was burned as an expression of worship to God. In those Christian churches that have an altar it is thought of as representing the sacrifice of Christ on the cross for our sins or as a communion table where we commune with Christ.

Amen. A word used to express agreement: "So be it."

Amistad. A ship used illegally to transport Mende people from Sierra Leone, Africa, for the slave trade in 1839. The name means "Friendship." The Mende, with support from abolitionists, won back their freedom in a famous Supreme Court trial with John Quincy Adams as their attorney.

Angel. A good spirit; messenger of God.

Anthem. A sacred composition for a choir, with words usually from the Bible.

Apostle. One who is sent out to preach the gospel; a missionary.

Ascension Day. The fortieth day after Jesus' resurrection; commemorates when his disciples saw him for the last time.

Ash Wednesday. The first day of Lent.

Association. A group of United Church of Christ congregations in a given area that organize to work together.

Atonement. At-one-ment; reconciliation between people and God through Christ.

B

Baptism. The ceremony through which a person becomes a Christian and comes into the Christian church; the sacred act by which God receives those who have repented of their sins and desire new life in Christ Jesus and in which the Holy Spirit guides people into full Christian life.

Begotten. Brought into being.

Benediction. A blessing pronounced by the minister at the close of a service of worship or at other times when God's blessing is asked for.

Benevolent. Kind; charitable; to wish others well and bring happiness to them.

Bible. The book made up of writings accepted by Christians as inspired by God and having divine authority; the Scriptures of the Old and New Testaments.

Bless. To consecrate; to make holy.

Blessed. Happy.

Blessing. A gift from God; the benediction, a prayer of thanks for a meal.

Born again. Beginning a new life based on acceptance of Christ as Savior and Lord.

Budget. A list of the things a church needs and for which money must be spent.

C

Candelabra. Large ornamental candlesticks having several branches.

Catechism. A set of questions put to candidates for membership in the church and the answers to be given to those questions; the book containing the questions and answers.

Cathedral. A church containing a bishop's chair.

Catholic. Universal, applying to the whole Christian church.

Chalice. The cup used for wine (or grape juice) in the Lord's Supper.

Chancel. The area surrounding the altar or communion table in a church.

Charge. One or more congregations served by one pastor.

Choir. An organized group of singers, usually in a church.

Christen. To make a Christian through baptism; to baptize infants, to give a name to.

Christian. A follower of Christ; one who accepts Christ as Lord and Savior and follows Jesus' teachings.

Church. A building set aside for worship; a congregation; a body of believers holding the same creed and following the same practices, as in a denomination; the community of all believers in Christ.

Church House. The name of our denomination's principal headquarters in Cleveland, Ohio.

Clergy. Men and women who have been ordained to the service of God by the Christian church.

Collegium of Officers. The five persons elected by General Synod to lead the Covenanted Ministries of the United Church of Christ, including the General Minister and President.

Commandment. An order given by God.

Communicant. One who partakes of the sacrament of the Lord's Supper.

Communion. A full spiritual relationship between people; participation in the sacrament of the Lord's Supper, ordinarily used with holy and capitalized in this sense; a denomination.

Conceived. Brought into life or existence.

Conference. A regional or state organization of churches.

Confession. An admission of wrongdoing or sin; a statement of belief.

Confirmation. An act of the church in which a person who has been baptized as a child confirms his or her vows, expresses his or her own faith, and is admitted to the full responsibilities of membership in the Christian church.

Conscience. The sense or consciousness of right or wrong; an inner voice that impels us to do right in harmony with God's will.

Consecrate. To declare sacred or holy; to dedicate or set apart for the service or worship of God.

Consistory. The governing body of a congregation; called the church council in some churches.

Conversion. A change in belief or conviction; turning from a sinful to a godly way of life.

Covenant. A solemn agreement between two or more people; an agreement between God and people.

Covenante Ministries. The four ministries or agencies of the national setting of the denomination whose executives are elected by General Synod. They are: Office of General Ministries, Justice and Witness Ministries, Wider Church Ministries and Local Church Ministries.

Covet. To desire strongly something that belongs to another.

Creed. A statement of belief.

The Cup. Often used in place of the word wine in speaking of the communion elements.

D

Deacon. A lay minister of the church who looks after its welfare.

Debts. Often used in place of trespasses in the Lord's Prayer; sins or wrongdoings.

Decalogue. The Ten Commandments.

Dedicate. To set apart to the service or the worship of God.

Denomination. A church body made up of congregations that have the same beliefs and the same type of church government.

Devil. The spirit of evil.

Disciple. A pupil; a follower of Christ.

Divine. Pertaining to God.

Doxology. A hymn or chant in praise of God; frequently refers to the one beginning "Praise God from whom all blessings flow."

E

Easter. The day on which we celebrate the resurrection of Christ.

Ecclesiastical. Having to do with the church.

Ecumenical. The whole inhabited earth, worldwide and, also, a movement of the divided churches toward visible unity without requiring uniformity.

Elder. An officer of the church who helps the pastor in caring for the spiritual life of the members. (In some congregations, this is the deacon's role.)

Elements. The bread and wine (or grape juice) used in Holy Communion.

Epiphany. The season of the church year that celebrates the coming of the Magi as the revelation of Christ to the Gentiles.

Eternal Life. Continuing community with God in this life and after death.

Eucharist. The sacrament of the Lord's Supper.

Evangelical. Contained in the four Gospels; a Protestant denomination holding certain beliefs.

Evangelism. Telling the good news of God's redeeming love in Christ.

Evil. Morally bad; contrary to divine law.

The Evil One. The devil; Satan.

F

Faith. Belief and trust in God.

Fellowship. Communion; an organization of Christians in the church.

Flock. A congregation whose leader is a pastor, or shepherd.

Font. The basin containing water for baptism.

G

Gloria in Excelsis. Latin for "Glory in the highest."

Gloria Patri. Latin for "Glory be to the Father."

Glory. Honor and praise given to God in worship.

Good Friday. The Friday before Easter Sunday; marks the day when Jesus was crucified. It is called Good Friday because of the new life won for us in Jesus' death.

Gospel. The good news of God's love in Christ; one of the four New Testament books that deal with the life and teachings of Jesus.

Grace. Divine mercy, love, and forgiveness, granted without any consideration of what one really deserves; a prayer of blessing or thanks offered at mealtime.

H

Hades. A Greek word for the abode of the dead; the place of departed spirits.

Hallowed. Blessed; holy; to be held in reverence.

Hell. A word for the abode of the dead; the place of punishment for sins committed during life.

Holy Communion. Another name for the Lord's Supper.

Holy Ghost, or Holy Spirit. The third Person of the Trinity who is ever present to guide us in the way of God.

Hymn. A song of praise, adoration, or prayer to God.

I

Idol. An image made to represent God and used as an object of worship.

Idolatry. Worship of an idol; excessive love or veneration for anything.

Immersion. Baptism by submerging a person in water.

Incarnation. Becoming flesh or human; the coming of God in the person of Jesus.

Intercession. Praying for another person or pleading for someone.

Invocation. Calling on God at the beginning of a service.

K

Kingdom of God (or heaven). See Realm of God.

L

Laity. Literally means "the people" and usually refers to all church members except the ordained clergy.

Lectern. A reading desk from which the Scriptures are read.

Lectionary. A schedule of readings from the Bible for use on assigned Sundays and special days in the calendar of the church year to enable Christians to read the Bible in common.

Lent. The season of the church year leading up to Easter.

Lord's Supper, or Holy Communion. The sacrament instituted by Christ through which we remember his life and his death on the cross for us and through which we receive from him new life.

M

Martyr (Witness). One who voluntarily suffered death for refusing to renounce Christ.

Maundy Thursday. The day before Good Friday when the Last Supper was held.

Mercy. Forgiveness; love that overlooks harm that has been done to one.

Minister. One authorized to conduct Christian worship, preach and teach the gospel, administer the sacraments, and exercise pastoral care and leadership.Missionary. One who is sent to preach the gospel, to teach, and to heal in the name of Christ.

N

Narthex. The part of the church that leads into the main part; the vestibule.

Nave. The main part of the church where the people sit.

Newness of Life. The continual change of mind and action for the better.

O

Omnipotent. All-powerful.

Omnipresent. Present everywhere.

Omniscient. All-wise; all-knowing.

Ordination. The consecration of someone as a Christian minister.

Our Church's Wider Mission. The work the United Church of Christ does in America and throughout the world for which people in the local churches con-tribute money.

P

Parish. The area in which the members of a congregation live.

Pastor. The minister in charge of a congregation; from the Latin word meaning "shepherd," therefore one who leads and takes care of the flock as a shepherd cares for sheep.

Pentecost. The fiftieth day after Easter; Whitsunday.

Petition. A request; that part of a prayer in which we ask God for something.

Prayer. Speaking, listening, and responding to God; being linked up in communication with others.

Prophet. One inspired by God to speak in God's name.

Protestant. A person who belongs to one of the churches that has grown out of the Reformation begun by Luther, Zwingli, Calvin, and others.

Providence. Divine guidance or care. Another word for God.

Pulpit. A raised platform, sometimes enclosed, where the minister stands while preaching.

Q

The Quick. The living.

R

Rabbi. A Hebrew word meaning "master" or "teacher."

Realm of God. A way of life in which the rule of God as revealed in Jesus Christ is accepted.

Reconciliation. Bringing back harmony after a misunderstanding; returning to community with God after sin has brought about separation.

Redeemer. One who rescues or delivers another from slavery by paying the purchase price; Christ, who rescues and delivers people from the slavery of sin and the punishment that would ordinarily follow on their breaking of God's law.

Reformation. Changing into a new and improved form; the religious movement of the sixteenth century that changed the church for the better and resulted in the formation of various Protestant churches.

Regeneration. The act of being spiritually reborn.

Remission of Sin. The forgiveness of sin; pardon.

Repentance. Feeling sorry for what one has done wrong and resolving to change one's life according to God's will.

Reredos. The screen or decorated part of the wall behind the altar.

Resurrection. Becoming alive again, as in Jesus' rising from the dead.

Revelation. God's sharing of identity, will, and purpose.

Reverence. A feeling of deep respect for what is sacred.

Revision. A revised edition (as of the Bible); a new, improved, or up-to-date version.

Right Hand of God. Position of honor and power in relation to God.

Righteous. Doing that which is right; free from wrong or sin.

Rite. A ritual, or a prescribed form of conducting a religious ceremony, as the rite of confirmation or marriage.

S

Sabbath. The seventh day of the week (Saturday) when the people of the Old Testament rested and worshiped God; sometimes used for Sunday.

Sacrament. A religious ceremony, distinguished from a rite in that it was instituted by Christ; Baptism and the Lord's Supper.

Sacrifice. An offering to God; giving oneself for another, as in Christ's giving of himself to save all people.

Salvation. The saving of people from the spiritual consequences of sin; especially, the deliverance from sin through Christ's sacrifice; freedom from sin and community with God. The word literally means "wholeness."

Sanctification. The process whereby God brings the believer to a righteous life.

Sanctuary. A consecrated place; the part of a church where the congregation meets for worship.

Satan. The devil.

Scripture. A sacred writing.

The Scriptures. The Bible.

Sermon. A discourse by a minister, based on a passage of scripture, for the purpose of religious instruction and inspiration.

Sin. An offense against God; a breaking of the relationship between God and people.

Soul. The essential self; the deep spirit in people.

Spirit. The breath of life; the soul; the Holy Spirit.

Stewardship. The good management of one's time, talents, and possessions in accordance with the will of God; thinking of all one has as a sacred trust to be used in service for God and humanity.

Swear. To utter a solemn declaration, calling on God to witness to the truth of the statement; to use God's name carelessly; to curse.

Synod. A church assembly or council.

T

Temptation. That which tempts, especially to do evil; that by which one is tested or tried.

Testament. A solemn agreement or covenant; one of the two main divisions of the Bible—the one being the result of the covenant made between God and the Israelites on Mount Sinai; the other, of the covenant made through Christ.

Theology. The knowledge of God; the study of religion and religious ideas.

Tithe. A tenth part; giving a tenth of one's income to God's work.

Translation. A version of the Bible changed from one language into another.

Trespasses. Often used in place of debts in the Lord's Prayer; sins or wrongdoings.

Trinity. God in three persons; Father, Son, and Holy Spirit (or Creator, Redeemer, and Sustainer); the eighth Sunday after Easter.

Triune. Three in one; one God in three persons.

U

Universal. Including all people on earth.

V

Version. A particular translation of the Bible.

Virgin. A pure, unmarried woman; Mary, the mother of Jesus.

W

The Way. A name given to Christianity in the early days.

Whitsunday. The fiftieth day after Easter; Pentecost.

Word of God. The truth of God revealed in the writings of the Bible and in Jesus Christ.

Worship. Honoring God; the act whereby a believer enters into communion with God.

Special Projects

The Covenanted Ministries of the United Church of Christ and a number of conferences support various specialized ministries at home and abroad.

Special projects are often undertaken with the cooperation of other denominations or voluntary agencies. They include special urban ministries, educational projects, rural and community development projects, and efforts to help people organize for a better life. For further information, contact the executive minister of any of the Covenanted Ministries or, for volunteer services, contact the Executive of Volunteer Ministries of Wider Church Ministries at 700 Prospect Avenue East, Cleveland, Ohio 44115-1100.

The Council for Health and Human Service Ministries

In 1961, four years after the formation of the United Church of Christ, the Council for Health and Welfare Services was organized to plan a program of health and welfare services.

Recognizing the necessity to be more directly involved with implementing the UCC's health and welfare programs, the council incorporated in 1982 and changed its name to the Council for Health and Human Services Ministries (CHHSM). The council oversees services to the elderly; services to children, youths, and families; acute health care services; and services to persons with disabilities. For more information contact CHHSM at 216-736-2250.

Academies, Colleges, Universities, and Seminaries

Andover Newton Theological School (1807), Newton Centre, MA
Bangor Theological Seminary (1814), Bangor, ME
Beloit College (1846), Beloit, WI
Carleton College (1866), Northfield, MN
Catawba College (1851), Salisbury, NC
Cedar Crest College (1867), Allentown, PA
Chicago Theological Seminary (1855), Chicago, IL
Deaconess College of Nursing (1889), St. Louis, MO
Defiance College, The (1850), Defiance, OH
Dillard University (1869), New Orleans, LA
Doane College (1872), Crete, NE

Drury College (1873), Springfield, MO
Eden Theological Seminary (1850), St. Louis, MO
Elmhurst College (1871), Elmhurst, IL
Elon College (1889), Elon College, NC
Fisk University (1865), Nashville, TN
Franklin and Marshall College (1787), Lancaster, PA
Grinnell College (1846), Grinnell, IA
Hartford Seminary (1834), Hartford, CT
Harvard University Divinity School (1811), Cambridge, MA
Heidelberg College (1850), Tiffin, OH
Hood College (1893), Frederick, MD
Howard University School of Divinity (1867), Washington, DC
Huston-Tillotson College (1952), Austin, TX
Illinois College (1829), Jacksonville, IL
Interdenominational Theological Center (1958), Atlanta, GA
Lakeland College (1862), Sheboygan, WI
Lancaster Theological Seminary (1825), Lancaster, PA
LeMoyne-Owen College (1871), Memphis, TN
Massanutten Academy (1899), Woodstock, VA
Mercersburg Academy (1836), Mercersburg, PA
Northland College (1892), Ashland, WI
Olivet College (1844), Olivet, MI
Pacific School of Religion (1866), Berkeley, CA
Pacific University (1849), Forest Grove, OR
Ripon College (1851), Ripon, WI
Rocky Mountain College (1883), Billings, MT
Seminario Evangelico de Puerto Rico (1919), San Juan, PR
Talladega College (1867), Talladega, AL
Tougaloo College (1869), Tougaloo, MS
Union Theological Seminary (1836), New York, NY
United Theological Seminary of the Twin Cities (1962), New Brighton, MN
Ursinus College (1869), Collegeville, PA
Vanderbilt University Divinity School (1875), Nashville, TN
Westminster College of Salt Lake City (1875), Salt Lake City, UT
Yale University Divinity School (1822), New Haven, CT

Notes

Chapter 6. About Jesus

1. Georgia Harkness, *Understanding the Christian Faith* (Nashville: Abingdon Press, 1992).

2. Gerald Early, ed., *My Soul's High Song: The Collected Writings of Countee Cullen, Voice of the Harlem Renaissance,* © 1991 by The Amistad Research Center. Used by permission.

Chapter 9. What We Believe

1. Arthur Cushman McGiffert, T*he Apostles' Creed: Its Origin, Its Purpose, and Its Historical Interpretation* (New York: Charles Scribner's Sons, 1902).

Chapter 19. The Sacraments

1. Joseph Cullen Ayer, *A Source Book for Ancient Church History* (New York: Charles Scribner's Sons, 1913). © 1913 by Charles Scribner's Sons; copyright renewed 1941 by Joseph Cullen Ayer, Jr. Used by permission.

2. United Church of Christ, *Book of Worship* (New York: United Church of Christ Office for Church Life and Leadership, 1986), 135. Used by permission.